THE WORLD'S GREAT SERMONS

L. BEECHER TO BUSHNELL

Volume IV

Compiled by

GRENVILLE KLEISER

With an Introduction by

LEWIS O. BRASTOW

First published in 1908

This edition published by Read Books Ltd.
Copyright © 2019 Read Books Ltd.
This book is copyright and may not be
reproduced or copied in any way without
the express permission of the publisher in writing

British Library Cataloguing-in-Publication Data
A catalogue record for this book is available
from the British Library

CONTENTS

4

BUSHNELL
Unconscious Influence

"The Lord Jesus Christ is the great Friend to whom we must all look for help, both for time and eternity."

—JOHN CHARLES RYLE

PREFACE

The aim in preparing this work has been to bring together the best examples of the products of the pulpit through the Christian centuries, and to present these masterpieces in attractive and convenient form. It is believed that they will be found valuable as instruction to ministers of to-day. They should also be helpful to others who, tho not preachers, yet seek reading of this kind for the upbuilding of personal character and for strengthening their Christian faith.

The sermons have been chosen in some cases for their literary and rhetorical excellences, but in every case for their helpfulness in solving some of the problems of Christian living. No two persons are likely to agree upon "the best" of anything, and readers will probably wish in particular instances that some other clergymen or sermons had been included. It is confidently believed, however, that the list here given is fairly representative of the preaching that characterized the age to which each sermon respectively belongs.

While some of the sermons of the early centuries may not seem exactly fitted to modern needs, it is thought that those presented will repay careful perusal, since they each contain a distinct message for later generations. Moreover, a comparison extending over the whole field of sermonic literature, such as the preacher may make with this collection before him, should prove most valuable as showing what progress and changes have come over homiletic matter and methods. Such a comparison should in fact throw much light on the spirit and conditions of various homiletic periods.

In choosing sermons by living preachers considerable difficulty has been found, not only in deciding upon sermons, but upon preachers. The list might have been extended indefinitely. Whenever possible the preacher, when living, has himself been consulted as to what he considered his most representative sermon.

Thanks are due, and are hereby acknowledged, to numerous clergymen, publishers, librarians, and others who have generously assisted the compiler in this undertaking. Most grateful acknowledgment is also made to the Rev. Epiphanius Wilson and the Rev. W.C. Stiles for valuable editorial assistance.

GRENVILLE KLEISER.
New York City, October, 1908.

INTRODUCTION

Collections of sermons by noted preachers of different periods are not an altogether uncommon contribution to literature. Italy, Germany, Holland, France, Great Britain and the United States have in this way furnished copious illustrations of the gifts of their illustrious preachers. Such treasures are found in the Latin and even in the Greek Church. Protestant communions especially, in line with the supreme significance which they attach to the work of the pulpit, have thus sought to magnify the calling and to perpetuate the memory and the influence of their distinguished sons. Still more comprehensive attempts have been made to collate the products of representative preachers in different Protestant communions, and thus to bring into prominence various types of sermonic literature. It is in this way that the Christian world has come to know its pulpit princes and to value their achievements.

The collection contained in the volumes before us is, however, more varied and comprehensive, reaching as it does from the fourth to the twentieth century, than any collection known to the writer. In the selection Professor Kleiser has brought to his task a personal knowledge of homiletic literature that is the product of much observation and study during many years, and an enthusiasm for his work that has been fostered by close intercourse in professional service with preachers and theological students. He has had the assistance also of men whose acquaintance with homiletic literature is very extensive, whose critical judgments are sound and reliable and who may be regarded as experts in this branch of knowledge. These volumes, therefore, may be accepted as a judiciously selected collection of sermons by many of the most notable preachers of the ancient and modern Christian world. Their value as illustrating varieties of gift, diversities of method, racial, national and ecclesiastical peculiarities, and above all progress in the science and art of preaching, may well be recognized even by a generation that is likely to regard anything that is more than twenty-four hours old as obsolete.

Lewis O. Brastow.
Yale University, New Haven, Conn.,
October, 1908.

LYMAN BEECHER

THE GOVERNMENT OF GOD DESIRABLE

BIOGRAPHICAL NOTE

Lyman Beecher was born in New Haven, Conn., in 1775. He graduated from Yale in 1797, and in 1798 took charge of the Presbyterian Church at Easthampton, Long Island. He first attracted attention by his sermon on the death of Alexander Hamilton, and in 1810 became pastor of the Congregational Church at Litchfield, Conn. In the course of a pastorate of 16 years, he preached a remarkable series of sermons on temperance and became recognized as one of the foremost pulpit orators of the country. In 1826 he went to Boston as pastor of the Hanover Street Congregational Church. Six years later he became president of the Lane Theological Seminary in Ohio, an office he retained for twenty years. In 1852 he returned to Boston and subsequently retired to the house of his son, Henry Ward Beecher, where he died in 1863. His public utterances, whether platform or pulpit, were carefully elaborated. They were delivered extemporaneously and sparkled with wit, were convincing by their logic, and conciliating by their shrewd common sense.

LYMAN BEECHER

1775-1863

THE GOVERNMENT OF GOD DESIRABLE

Thy will be done in earth as it is in heaven.—Matthew vi., 10.

In this passage we are instructed to pray that the world may be governed, and not abandoned to the miseries of unrestrained sin; that God Himself would govern, and not another; and that God would administer the government of the world, in all respects, according to His own pleasure. The passage is a formal surrender to God of power and dominion over the earth, as entire as His dominion is in His heaven. The petition, therefore, "Thy will be done," contains the doctrine:

That it is greatly to be desired that God should govern the world, and dispose of men, in all respects, entirely according to His own pleasure.

The truth of this doctrine is so manifest, that it would seem to rank itself in the number of self-evident propositions, incapable of proof clearer than its own light, had not experience taught that, of all truths, it is the most universally and bitterly controverted. Plain as it is, it has occasioned more argument than any other doctrine, and, by argument merely, has gained fewer proselytes; for it is one of those controversies in which the heart decides wholly, and argument, strong or feeble, is alike ineffectual.

This consideration would present, on the threshold, a hopeless impediment to further progress, did we not know, also, that arguments a thousand times repeated, and as often resisted, may at length become mighty through God, to the casting down of imaginations, and every high thing that exalteth itself against the knowledge of God. I shall, therefore, suggest several considerations, to confirm this most obvious truth, that it is desirable that God should govern the world entirely according to His own good pleasure.

1. It is desirable that God should govern the world, and dispose of all events, according to His pleasure, because He knows perfectly in what manner it is best that the world should be governed.

The best way of disposing of men and their concerns is that which will effectually illustrate the glory of God. The glory of God is His benevolence, and His natural attributes for the manifestation of it, and sun of the moral universe, the light and life of His kingdom. All the blessedness of the intelligent creation arises, and ever will arise, from the manifestation and apprehension of the glory of God. It was to manifest this glory that the worlds were created. It was that there might be creatures to behold and enjoy God, that His dominions were peopled with intelligent beings. And it is that His holy subjects may see and enjoy Him, that He upholds and governs the universe. The entire importance of our world, therefore, and of men and their concerns, is relative, and is great or small only as we are made to illustrate the glory of God. How this important end shall be most effectually accomplished none but Himself is able to determine. He, only, knows how so to order things as that the existence of every being, and every event, shall answer the purpose of its creation, and from the rolling of a world to the fall of a sparrow shall conspire to increase the exhibitions of the divine character, and expand the joy of the holy universe.

An inferior intelligence at the helm of government might conceive very desirable purposes of benevolence, and still be at a loss as to the means most fit and effectual to accomplish them. But, with God, there is no such deficiency. In Him, the knowledge which discovered the end discovers also, with unerring wisdom, the most appropriate means to bring it to pass. He is wise in heart; He hath established the world by His wisdom and stretched out the heavens by His discretion. And is He not wise enough to be intrusted with the government of the world? Who, then, shall be His counsellor? Who shall supply the deficiencies of His skill? Oh, the presumption of vain man! and, oh! the depths both of the wisdom and knowledge of God!

2. It is desirable that God should govern the world according to His own pleasure, because He is entirely able to execute His purposes.

A wise politician perceives, often, both the end and the means; and is still unable to bring to pass his counsels, because the means, though wise, are beyond his control. But God is as able to execute as He is to plan. Having chosen the end, and selected the means, his counsels stand. He is the Lord God omnipotent. The whole universe is a storehouse of means; and when He speaks every intelligence and every atom flies to execute His pleasure. The omnipotence of God, in giving efficacy to His government, inspires and perpetuates the ecstasy of heaven. "And a voice came out from the throne, saying, Praise our God. And I heard as it were the voice of a great multitude, and as the voice of many waters, and as the voice of many thunderings, saying Alleluia, the Lord God omnipotent reigneth." What will that man do in heaven, who is afraid and reluctant to commit to God the government of the earth? And what will become of those who, unable to frustrate His counsels, murmur and rebel against His providence?

3. It is desirable that God should govern the world according to His pleasure, because the pleasure of God is always good.

The angels who kept not their first estate, and many wicked men, have great knowledge, and skill, and power: and yet, on these accounts, are only the more terrible; because they employ these mighty faculties to do evil. And the government of God, were He a being of malevolence, armed as He is with skill and power, would justly fill the universe with dismay. But, as it is, brethren, "let not your hearts be troubled." With God there is no perversion of attributes. He is as good as He is wise and powerful. God is love! Love is that glory of God which He has undertaken to express to His intelligent creation in His works. The sole object of the government of God, from beginning to end, is, to express His benevolence. His eternal decrees, of which so many are afraid, are nothing but the plan which God has devised to express His benevolence, and to make His kingdom as vast and as blest as His own infinite goodness desires. It was to show His glory—to express, in action, His benevolence—that He created all the worlds that roll, and rejoice, and speak His name, through the regions of space. It is to accomplish the same blest design, that He upholds, and places under law, every intelligent being, and directs every event, causing every movement, in every world, to fall in, in its appointed time and place, and to unite in promoting the grand result—the glory of God, and the highest good of His kingdom. And is there a mortal, who, from this great system of blest government, would wish this earth to be an exception? What sort of beings must those be who are afraid of a government administered by infinite benevolence, to express, so far as it can be expressed, the infinite goodness of God? I repeat the question,—What kind of characters must those be who feel as if they had good reason to fear a government the sole object of which is to express the immeasurable goodness of God?

4. It is greatly to be desired that God should govern the world according to His pleasure, because it is His pleasure to rule as a moral governor.

A moral government is a government exercised over free agents, accountable beings; a government of laws, administered by motives.

The importance of such a government below is manifest from the consideration, that it is in His moral government, chiefly, that the glory of God is displayed.

The superintendence of an empty world, or a world of mere animals, would not exhibit, at all, the moral character of God. The glory of God, shining in His law, could never be made manifest, and the brighter glory of God, as displayed in the

18

gospel, must remain forever hid; and all that happiness of which we are capable, as moral beings, the joys of religion below, and the boundless joys of heaven above, would be extinguished, in a moment, by the suspension of the divine moral government.

Will any pretend that the Almighty cannot maintain a moral government on earth, if He governs according to His own pleasure? Can He wield the elements, and control, at His pleasure, every work of His hands, but just the mind of man? Is the most noble work of God—that which is the most worthy of attention, and in reference to which all beside is upheld and governed—itself wholly unmanageable? Has Omnipotence formed minds, which, the moment they are made, escape from His hands, and defy the control of their Maker? Has the Almighty erected a moral kingdom which He cannot govern without destroying its moral nature? Can He only watch, and mend, and rectify, the lawless wanderings of mind? Has He filled the earth with untamed and untamable spirits, whose wickedness and rebellion He can merely mitigate, but cannot control? Does He superintend a world of madmen, full of darkness and disorder, cheered and blest by no internal pervading government of His own? Are we bound to submit to all events, as parts of the holy providence of God; and yet, is there actually no hand of God controlling the movements of the moral world? But if the Almighty can, and if he does, govern the earth as a part of His moral kingdom, is there any method of government more safe and wise than that which pleases God? Can there be a better government? We may safely pray, then, "Thy will be done in earth as it is in heaven," without fearing at all the loss of moral agency; for all the glory of God, in His Law and Gospel, and all the eternal manifestations of glory to principalities and powers in heavenly places, depend wholly upon the fact, that men, though living under the government of God, and controlled according to His pleasure, are still entirely free, and accountable for all the deeds done in the body. There could be no justice in punishment and no condescension, no wisdom, no mercy, in the glorious gospel, did not the government

19

of God, though administered according to His pleasure, include and insure the accountable agency of man.

Seeing, therefore, that all the glory of God, which He ever proposes to manifest to the intelligent creation, is to be made known by the Church, and is to shine in the face of Jesus Christ, and is to depend upon the perfect consistency of the moral government of God with human freedom, we have boundless assurance that, among His absolute, immutable, eternal purposes, one, and a leading one, is, so to govern the world according to His counsels, that, if men sin, there shall be complete desert of punishment, and boundless mercy in their redemption.

5. It is greatly to be desired that God should rule in the earth according to His pleasure, because it is His pleasure to govern the world in mercy, by Jesus Christ.

The government is in the hand of a Mediator, by whom God is reconciling the world to Himself, not imputing their trespasses to them that believe. Mercy is the bestowment of pardon upon the sinful and undeserving. Now, mankind are so eminently sinful, that no government but one administered in infinite mercy, could afford the least consolation. Had any being but the God of mercy sat upon the throne, or any will but His will prevailed, there would have been no plan of redemption, and no purposes of election, to perplex and alarm the wicked. There would have been but one decree, and that would have been, destruction to the whole race of man. Are any reluctant to be entirely in the hands of God? Are they afraid to trust Him to dispose of soul and body, for time and eternity? Let them surrender their mercies, then, and go out naked from that government which feeds, protects and comforts them. Let them give up their Bibles, and relinquish the means of grace, and the hopes of glory, and descend and make their bed in hell, where they have long since deserved to be, and where they long since would have been, if God had not governed the world according to His own good pleasure. If they would escape the evils which they fear from the hand of God, let them abandon the blessings they receive from it, and they will soon discover whether the absolute dominion of God, and their dependence upon Him, be, in reality, a ground of murmuring and alarm. Our only hope of heaven arises from being entirely in the hands of God. Our destruction could not be made more certain than it would be were we to be given up to our own disposal, or to the disposal of any being but God. Would sinful mortals change their own hearts? Could the combined universe, without God, change the depraved affections of men? Surely, then, we have cause for unceasing joy, that we are in the hands of God; seeing He is a God of mercy, and has decreed to rule in mercy, and actually is administering the government of the world in mercy, by Jesus Christ.

We have nothing to fear, from the entire dominion of God, which we should not have cause equally to fear, as outcasts from the divine government; but we have everything to hope, while He rules the earth according to His most merciful pleasure. The Lord reigneth; let the earth rejoice, let the multitude of the isles be glad. It is of the Lord's mercies that we are not consumed, because His compassions fail not.

6. It is greatly to be desired that God should dispose of mankind according to His pleasure, because, if He does so, it is certain that there will be no injustice done to anyone.

He will do no injustice to His holy kingdom by any whom He saves. He will bring none to heaven who are not holy, and prepared for heaven. He will bring none there in any way not consistent with His perfections, and the best good of His kingdom; none in any way but that prescribed in the gospel, the way of faith in Jesus Christ, of repentance for sin, and of good works as the constituted fruit and evidence of faith.

Earthly monarchs have their favorites, whom, if guilty of a violation of the laws, they will often interpose to save, although the welfare of the kingdom requires their punishment. But God has no such favorites—He is no respecter of persons: He spared not the angels: and upon the earth distinctions of intellect, or wealth, or honor, will have no effect; he only that believeth shall be saved. The great and the learned shall not be obtruded upon heaven without holiness because they are great or learned; and the humble and contrite shall not be excluded because they are poor, or ignorant, or obscure. God has provided a way for all men to return to Him. He has opened the door of their prison, and set open before them a door of admission into the kingdom of His dear Son; and commanded and entreated them to abandon their dreary abode, and come into the glorious liberty of the sons of God. But all, with one consent, refuse to comply. Each prefers his own loathsome dwelling to the building of God, and chooses, stedfastly, the darkness of his own dungeon, to the light of God's kingdom. But, as God has determined that the redemption of His Son shall not be unavailing through human obstinacy, so He hath chosen, in Christ, multitudes which no man can number, that they should be holy and without blame before Him in love. And in bringing these sons and daughters to glory, through sanctification of the Spirit, and belief of the truth, He will introduce not one whom all the inhabitants of heaven will not hail joyfully, as the companion of their glory. And if God does in the earth just as He pleases, He will make willing, and obedient, and bring to heaven, just those persons who it was most desirable should come. And He will bring just as many obstinate rebels to abandon their prison, and enter cheerfully His kingdom, as infinite wisdom, goodness, and mercy, see fit and desire. He will not mar His glory, or the happiness of His kingdom, by bringing in too many, nor by omitting to bring in enough. His redeemed kingdom, as to the number and the persons who compose it, and the happiness included in it, will be such as shall be wholly satisfactory to God, and to every subject of His kingdom.

And if God governs according to His pleasure, He will do no injustice to His impenitent enemies. He will send to misery no harmless animals without souls—no mere machines—none who have done, or even attempted to do, as well as they could. He will leave to walk in their own way none who do not deserve to be left; and punish none for walking in it who did not walk therein knowingly, deliberately and with wilful obstinacy. He will give up to death none who did not choose death, and choose it with as entire freedom as Himself chooses holiness; and who did not deserve eternal punishment as truly as Himself deserves eternal praise. He will send to hell none who are not opposed to Him, and to holiness, and to heaven; none who are not, by voluntary sin and rebellion, unfitted for heaven, and fitted for destruction, as eminently as saints are prepared for glory. He will consign to perdition no poor, feeble, inoffensive beings, sacrificing one innocent creature to increase the happiness of another. He will cause the punishment of the wicked to illustrate His glory, and thus indirectly to promote the happiness of heaven. But God will not illumine heaven with His glory, and fill it with praise, by sacrificing helpless, unoffending creatures to eternal torment; nor will He doom to hell one whom He will not convince also, that he deserves to go thither. The justice of God, in the condemnation of the impenitent, will be as unquestionable, as His infinite mercy will be in the salvation of the redeemed.

If the will of God is done on earth, among men, there will be no more injustice done to the inhabitants of the earth than there is done to the blessed in heaven. Was it ever known—did any ever complain—was it ever conceived—that God was a tyrant, in heaven? Why, then, should we question the justice of His government on earth? Is He not the same God below as above? Are not all His attributes equally employed? Does He not govern for the same end, and will not His government below conspire to promote the same joyful end as His government above?

7. It is greatly to be desired that God should govern the world according to His pleasure, because His own infinite blessedness, as well as the happiness of His kingdom, depends upon His working all things according to the counsel of His own will.

Could the Almighty be prevented from expressing the benevolence of His nature, according to His purposes, His present boundless blessedness would become the pain of ungratified desire. God is love, and His happiness consists in the exercise and expression of it, according to His own eternal purpose, which He purposed in Christ Jesus before the world began. It is therefore declared, "The Lord hath made all things for himself;" that is, to express and gratify His infinite benevolence. The moral excellence of God does not consist in quiescent love, but in love active, bursting forth, and abounding. Nor does the divine happiness arise from the contemplation of idle perfections, but from perfections which comprehend boundless capacity, and activity in doing good.

From what has been said, we may be led to contemplate with satisfaction the infinite blessedness of God.

God is love! This is a disposition which, beyond all others, is happy in its own nature. He is perfect in love; there is, therefore, in His happiness no alloy. His love is infinite; and, of course, His blessedness is unbounded. If the little holiness existing in good men, though balanced by remaining sin, occasions, at times, unutterable joy, how blessed must God be, who is perfectly and infinitely holy! It is to be remembered, also, that the benevolence of God is at all times perfectly gratified. The universe which God has created and upholds, including what He has done, and what He will yet do, will be brought into a condition which will satisfy His infinite benevolence. The great plan of government which God has chosen, and which His power and wisdom will execute, will embrace as much good as in the nature of things is possible. He is not, like erring man, straitened and perplexed, through lack of knowledge or power. There is in Hisplan no defect, and in His execution no failure. God, therefore, is infinitely happy in His holiness, and in the expression of it which it pleases Him to make.

The revolt of angels, the fall of man, and the miseries of sin, do not, for a moment, interrupt the blessedness of God. They were not, to Him, unexpected events, starting up suddenly while the watchman of Israel slumbered. They were foreseen by God as clearly as any other events of His government, and have occasioned neither perplexity nor dismay. With infinite complacency He beholds still His unshaken counsels, and with almighty hand rolls on His undisturbed decrees. Surrounded by unnumbered millions, created by His hand, and upheld by His power, He shines forth, God over all, blest for ever. What an object of joyful contemplation, then, is the blessedness of God! It is infinite; His boundless capacity is full. It is eternal; He is God blest forever. The happiness of the created universe is but a drop—a drop to the mighty ocean of divine enjoyment. How delightful the thought, that in God there is such an immensity of joy, beyond the reach of vicissitude! When we look around below, a melancholy sensation pervades the mind. What miserable creatures! What a wretched world! But when, from this scene of darkness and misery, we look up to the throne of God, and behold Him, high above the darkness and miseries of sin, dwelling in light inaccessible and full of glory, the prospect brightens. If a few rebels, who refuse to love and participate in His munificence, are groping in darkness on His footstool, God is light, and in Him there is no darkness at all.

Those who are opposed to the decrees of God, and to His sovereignty, as displayed in the salvation of sinners, are enemies of God.

They are unwilling that His will should be done in earth as it is in heaven; for the decrees of God are nothing but His choice as to the manner in which He will govern His own kingdom. He did not enter upon His government to learn wisdom by experience. Before they were yet formed, His vast dominion lay open to His view; and before He took the reins of created empire, He saw in what manner it became Him to govern. His ways are everlasting. Known unto God are all His works from the beginning. To be opposed to the decrees of God, therefore, is to be unwilling that God should have any choice concerning the government of the world. And can those be willing that God should govern the world entirely according to His pleasure who object to His having any pleasure upon the subject? To object to the choice of God, with respect to the management of the world, because it is eternal, is to object to the existence of God. A God of eternal knowledge, without an eternal will or choice, would be a God without moral character.

To suppose that God did not know what events would exist in His kingdom, is to divest Him of omniscience. To suppose that He did know, and did not care,—had no choice, no purpose,—is to blot out His benevolence, to nullify His wisdom and convert His power into infinite indolence. To suppose that He did know, and choose, and decree, and that events do not accord with His purposes, is to suppose that God has made a world which He can not govern; has undertaken a work too vast; has begun to build, but is not able to finish. But to suppose that God did, from the beginning, behold all things open and naked before Him, and that He did choose, with unerring wisdom and infinite goodness, how to govern His empire,—and yet at the same time, to employ heart, and head, and tongue, in continual opposition to this great and blessed truth,—is, most clearly, to cherish enmity to God and His government.

To object to the choice of God because it is immutable, is to cavil against that which constitutes its consummating excellence. Caprice is a most alarming feature in a bad government; but in a government absolutely perfect, none, surely, can object to its immutability, but those, who, if able, would alter it for the worse.

To say that, if God always knew how to govern so as to display His glory, and bless His kingdom, and always chooses thus to govern, there can be, therefore, no accountable agency in the conduct of His creatures, is to deny the possibility of a moral government, to contradict the express testimony of God; and this, too, at the expense of common sense, and the actual experience of every subject of His moral government on earth.

From the character of God, and the nature of His government, as explained in this discourse, may be inferred, the nature and necessity of unconditional submission to God.

Unconditional submission is an entire surrender of the soul to God, to be disposed of according to His pleasure,—occasioned by confidence in His character as God.

There are many who would trust the Almighty to regulate the rolling of worlds, and to rule in the armies of heaven, just as He pleases; and devils they would consign to His disposal, without the least hesitation; and their own nation, if they were sure that God would dispose of it according to their pleasure; even their own temporal concerns they would risk in the hands of God, could they know that all things would work together for their good; their souls, also, they would cheerfully trust to His disposal, for the world to come, if God would stipulate, at all events, to make them happy.

And to what does all this amount? Truly, that they care much about their own happiness, and their own will, but nothing at all about the will of God, and the welfare of His kingdom. He may decree, and execute His decrees, in heaven, and may turn its inhabitants into machines, or uphold their freedom, as He pleases; and apostate spirits are relinquished to their doom, whether just or unjust. It is only when the government of God descends to particulars, and draws near and enters their own selfish enclosures, and claims a right to dispose of them, and extends its influence to the unseen world, that selfishness and fear take the alarm. Has God determined how to dispose of my soul? Ah! that alters the case. If He can, consistently with freedom, govern angels, and devils, and nations, how can He govern individuals? How can He dispose of me according to His eternal purpose and I be free? Here reason, all-penetrating, and all-comprehensive, becomes weak; the clouds begin to collect, and the understanding, veiled by the darkness of the heart, can "find no end, in wandering mazes lost."

But if God has purposes of mercy in reserve for the sinner, he is convinced, at length, of his sin, and finds himself in an evil case. He reforms, prays, weeps, resolves, and re-resolves, regardless of the righteousness of Christ, and intent only to establish a righteousness of his own. But, through all his windings, sin cleaves to him, and the law, with its fearful curse, pursues him. Whither shall he flee? What shall he do? A rebel heart, that will not bow, fills him with despair. An angry God, who will not clear the guilty, fills him with terror. His strength is gone, his resources fail, his mouth is stopped. With restless anxiety, or wild amazement, he surveys the gloomy prospect. At length, amidst the wanderings of despair, the character of God meets his eye. It is new, it is amiable, and full of glory. Forgetful of danger, he turns aside to behold this great sight; and while he gazes, new affections awake in his soul, inspiring new confidence in God, and in His holy government. Now God appears qualified to govern, and now he is willing that He should govern, and willing himself to be in the hands of God, to be disposed of according to His pleasure. What is the occasion of this change? Has the divine character changed? There is no variableness with God. Did he, then, misapprehend the divine character? Was all this glory visible before? Or has a revelation of new truth been granted? There has been no new revelation. The character now admitted is the same which just before appeared so gloomy and terrible. What, then, has produced this alteration? Has a vision of angels appeared, to announce that God is reconciled? Has some sudden light burst upon him, in token of forgiveness? Has Christ been seen upon the cross, beckoning the sinner to come to Him? Has heaven been thrown open to his admiring eyes? Have enrapturing sounds of music stolen upon the ear, to entrance the soul? Has some text of Scripture been sent to whisper that his sins are forgiven, tho no repentance, nor faith, nor love, has dawned in his soul? And does he now submit, because God has given him assurance of personal safety? None of these. Considerations of personal safety are, at the time, out of the question. It is the uncreated, essential excellence of God, shining in upon the heart, which claims the attention, fixes the adoring eye, and fills the soul with love, and peace, and joy; and the act of submission is past, before the subject begins to reflect upon his altered views, with dawning hope of personal redemption.

The change produced, then, is the effect of benevolence,

raising the affections of the soul from the world, and resting them upon God. Holiness is now most ardently loved. This is seen to dwell in God and His kingdom, and to be upheld and perfected by His moral government. It is the treasure of the soul, and all the attributes of God stand pledged to protect it. The solicitude, therefore, is not merely, What will become of me? but, What, O Lord, will become of Thy glory, and the glory of Thy kingdom? And in the character of God, these inquiries are satisfactorily answered. If God be glorified, and His kingdom upheld and made happy, the soul is satisfied. There is nothing else to be anxious about; for individual happiness is included in the general good, as the drop is included in the ocean.

CHANNING

THE CHARACTER OF CHRIST

BIOGRAPHICAL NOTE

William Ellery Channing, the famous Unitarian divine, was born at Newport, R. I., in 1780. He took his degree at Harvard in 1798, studied theology and was ordained pastor of the Federal Street Church in Boston, 1803. He has been called the Apostle of Unitarianism, because he was first among the orthodox divines of New England to give Unitarianism a clear, dogmatic expression, as he did in a sermon preached at the ordination of Jared Sparks, in opposition to the current Calvinism of the day. But he hated the controversy in which the publication of his views involved him and professed in 1841, "I am little of a Unitarian and stand aloof from all but those who strive and pray for clearer light." He had made the acquaintance of Wordsworth and Coleridge on his visit to England, and the latter justly described him as one who had "the love of wisdom and the wisdom of love." He was a voluminous writer on theological and literary subjects and what he wrote was vigorous, of fastidious taste and fired with moral earnestness. He died in 1842.

CHANNING

1780-1842

THE CHARACTER OF CHRIST

This is my beloved Son, in whom I am well pleased.—
Matthew xvii., 5.

The character of Christ may be studied for various purposes.
It is singularly fitted to call forth the heart, to awaken love,
admiration, and moral delight. As an example it has no rival. As
an evidence of His religion perhaps it yields to no other proof;
perhaps no other has so often conquered unbelief. It is chiefly to
this last view of it that I now ask your attention. The character
of Christ is a strong confirmation of the truth of His religion.
As such I would now place it before you. I shall not, however,
think only of confirming your faith; the very illustrations which
I shall adduce for this purpose will show the claims of Jesus to
our reverence, obedience, imitation, and fervent love.

The more we contemplate Christ's character as exhibited in
the gospel, the more we shall be impressed with its genuineness
and reality. It was plainly drawn from the life. The narratives of
the evangelists bear the marks of truth perhaps beyond all other
histories. They set before us the most extraordinary being who
ever appeared on earth, and yet they are as artless as the stories
of childhood. The authors do not think of themselves. They have
plainly but one aim, to show us their Master; and they manifest
the deep veneration which He inspired by leaving Him to reveal
Himself, by giving us His actions and sayings without comment,
explanation, or eulogy.

You see in these narratives no varnishing, no high coloring, no attempts to make His actions striking or to bring out the beauties of His character. We are never pointed to any circumstance as illustrative of His greatness. The evangelists write with a calm trust in His character, with a feeling that it needed no aid from their hands, and with a deep veneration, as if comment or praise of their own were not worthy to mingle with the recital of such a life.

It is the effect of our familiarity with the history of Jesus that we are not struck by it as we ought to be. We read it before we are capable of understanding its excellence. His stupendous works become as familiar to us as the events of ordinary life, and His high offices seem as much matters of course as the common relations which men bear to each other.

On this account it is fit for the ministers of religion to do what the evangelists did not attempt, to offer comments on Christ's character, to bring out its features, to point men to its higher beauties, to awaken their awe by unfolding its wonderful majesty. Indeed, one of our most important functions as teachers is to give freshness and vividness to truths which have become worn, I had almost said tarnished, by long and familiar handling. We have to fight with the power of habit. Through habit men look on this glorious creation with insensibility, and are less moved by the all-enlightening sun than by a show of fireworks. It is the duty of a moral and religious teacher almost to create a new sense in men, that they may learn in what a world of beauty and magnificence they live. And so in regard to Christ's character; men become used to it until they imagine that there is something more admirable in a great man of their own day, a statesman or a conqueror, than in Him the latchet of whose shoes statesmen and conquerors are not worthy to unloose.

In this discourse I wish to show that the character of Christ, taken as a whole, is one which could not have entered the thoughts of man, could not have been imagined or feigned; that it bears every mark of genuineness and truth; that it ought therefore to be acknowledged as real and of divine origin.

It is all-important, my friends, if we would feel the force of this argument, to transport ourselves to the times when Jesus lived. We are very apt to think that He was moving about in such a city as this, or among a people agreeing with ourselves in modes of thinking and habits of life. But the truth is, he lived in a state of society singularly remote from our own.

Of all the nations the Jewish was the most strongly marked. The Jew hardly felt himself to belong to the human family. He was accustomed to speak of himself as chosen by God, holy, clean; whilst the Gentiles were sinners, dogs, polluted, unclean. His common dress, the phylactery on his brow or arm, the hem of his garment, his food, the ordinary circumstances of his life, as well as his temple, his sacrifices, his ablutions, all held him up to himself as a peculiar favorite of God, and all separated him from the rest of the world. With other nations he could not eat or marry. They were unworthy of his communion. Still, with all these notions of superiority he saw himself conquered by those whom he despised. He was obliged to wear the shackles of Rome, to see Roman legions in his territory, a Roman guard near his temple, and a Roman tax-gatherer extorting, for the support of an idolatrous government and an idolatrous worship, what he regarded as due only to God. The hatred which burned in the breast of the Jew toward his foreign oppressor perhaps never glowed with equal intenseness in any other conquered state.

He had, however, his secret consolation. The time was near, the prophetic age was at hand, when Judea was to break her chains and rise from the dust. Her long-promised king and deliverer was near, and was coming to wear the crown of universal empire. From Jerusalem was to go forth His law, and all nations were to serve the chosen people of God. To this conqueror the Jews indeed ascribed the office of promoting religion; but the religion of Moses, corrupted into an outward service, was to them the perfection of human nature. They clung to its forms with the whole energy of their souls. To the Mosaic institution they ascribed their distinction from all other nations. It lay at the foundation of their hopes of dominion. I believe no strength of prejudice ever equalled the intense attachment of the Jew to his peculiar national religion. You may judge of its power by the fact of its having been transmitted through so many ages, amidst persecution and sufferings which would have subdued any spirit but that of a Jew. You must bring these things to your mind. You must place yourselves in the midst of this singular people.

Among this singular people, burning with impatient expectation, appeared Jesus of Nazareth. His first words were, "Repent, for the kingdom of heaven is at hand." These words we hear with little emotion; but to the Jews, who had been watching for this kingdom for ages, and who were looking for its immediate manifestation, they must have been awakening as an earthquake. Accordingly we find Jesus thronged by multitudes which no building could contain. He repairs to a mountain, as affording him advantages for addressing the crowd. I see them surrounding Him with eager looks, and ready to drink in every word from His lips. And what do I hear? Not one word of Judea, of Rome, of freedom, of conquest, of the glories of God's chosen people, and of the thronging of all nations to the temple on Mount Zion.

Almost every word was a death-blow to the hopes and feelings which glowed through the whole people, and were consecrated under the name of religion. He speaks of the long-expected kingdom of heaven; but speaks of it as a felicity promised to, and only to be partaken of by, the humble and pure in heart. The righteousness of the Pharisees, that which was deemed the perfection of religion, and which the new deliverer was expected to spread far and wide, He pronounces worthless, and declares the kingdom of heaven, or of the Messiah, to be shut against all who do not cultivate a new, spiritual, and disinterested virtue.

Instead of war and victory He commands His impatient hearers to love, to forgive, to bless their enemies; and holds forth this spirit of benignity, mercy, peace, as the special badge of the people of the true Messiah. Instead of national interests and glories, he commands them to seek first a spirit of impartial charity and love, unconfined by the bounds of tribe or nation, and proclaims this to be the happiness and honor of the reign for which they hoped. Instead of this world's riches, which they expected to flow from all lands into their own, He commands them to lay up treasures in heaven, and directs them to an incorruptible, immortal life, as the true end of their being.

Nor is this all. He does not merely offer himself as a spiritual deliverer, as the founder of a new empire of inward piety and universal charity; He closes with language announcing a more mysterious office. "Many will say unto Me in that day, Lord, Lord, have we not prophesied in Thy name, and in Thy name done many wonderful works? And then will I profess unto them, I never knew you; depart from Me, ye that work iniquity." Here I meet the annunciation of a character as august as it must have been startling. I hear Him foretelling a dominion to be exercised in the future world. He begins to announce, what entered largely into His future teaching, that His power was not bounded to this earth. These words I better understand when I hear Him subsequently declaring that, after a painful death, He was to rise again and ascend to heaven, and there, in a state of preeminent power and glory, was to be the advocate and judge of the human race.

Such are some of the views given by Jesus, of His character and reign, in the Sermon on the Mount. Immediately afterwards I hear another lesson from Him, bringing out some of these truths still more strongly. A Roman centurion makes application to Him for the cure of a servant whom he particularly valued; and on expressing, in a strong manner, his conviction of the power of Jesus to heal at a distance, Jesus, according to the historian, "marvelled, and said to those that followed, Verily I say unto you, I have not found so great faith in Israel; and I say unto you, that many shall come from the east and west, and shall sit down with Abraham, and Isaac, and Jacob in the kingdom of heaven; but the children of the kingdom" (that is, the Jews) "shall be cast out."

Here all the hopes which the Jews had cherished of an exclusive or peculiar possession of the Messiah's kingdom were crushed; and the reception of the despised Gentile world to all His blessings, or, in other words, the extension of His pure religion to the ends of the earth, began to be proclaimed.

Here I pause for the present, and I ask you whether the character of Jesus be not the most extraordinary in history, and wholly inexplicable on human principles. Review the ground over which we have gone. Recollect that He was born and grew up a Jew in the midst of Jews, a people burning with one passion, and throwing their whole souls into the expectation of a national and earthly deliverer. He grew up among them in poverty, seclusion, and labors fitted to contract His thoughts, purposes, and hopes; and yet we find Him escaping every influence of education and society. We find Him as untouched by the feelings which prevailed universally around Him, which religion and patriotism concurred to consecrate, which the mother breathed into the ear of the child, and which the teacher of the synagog strengthened in the adult, as if He had been brought up in another world. We find Him conceiving a sublime purpose, such as had never dawned on sage or hero, and see Him possessed with a consciousness of sustaining a relation to God and mankind, and of being invested with powers in this world and the world to come, such as had never entered the human mind. Whence now, I ask, came the conception of this character?

Will any say it had its origin in imposture; that it was a fabrication of a deceiver? I answer, the character claimed by Christ excludes this supposition by its very nature. It was so remote from all the ideas and anticipations of the times, so unfit to awaken sympathy, so unattractive to the heathen, so exasperating to the Jew, that it was the last to enter the mind of an impostor. A deceiver of the dullest vision must have foreseen that it would expose him to bitter scorn, abhorrence, and persecution, and that he would be left to carry on his work alone, just as Jesus always stood alone and could find not an individual to enter into His spirit and design. What allurements an unprincipled, self-seeking man could find to such an enterprise, no common ingenuity can discover.

I affirm next that the sublimity of the character claimed by Christ forbids us to trace it to imposture. That a selfish, designing, depraved mind could have formed the idea and purpose of a work unparalleled in beneficence, in vastness, and in moral grandeur, would certainly be a strange departure from the laws of the human mind. I add, that if an impostor could have lighted on the conception of so sublime and wonderful a work as that claimed by Jesus, he could not, I say, he could not have thrown into his personation of it the air of truth and reality. The part would have been too high for him. He would have overacted it or fallen short of it perpetually. His true character would have rebelled against his assumed one. We should have seen something strained, forced, artificial, awkward, showing that he was not in his true sphere. To act up to a character so singular and grand, and one for which no precedent could be found, seems to me utterly impossible for a man who had not the true spirit of it, or who was only wearing it as a mask.

Now, how stands the case with Jesus? Bred a Jewish peasant or carpenter, He issues from obscurity, and claims for Himself a divine office, a superhuman dignity, such as had not been imagined; and in no instance does He fall below the character. The peasant, and still more the Jew, wholly disappears.

We feel that a new being, of a new order of mind, is taking a part in human affairs. There is a native tone of grandeur and authority in His teaching. He speaks as a being related to the whole human race. His mind never shrinks within the ordinary limits of human agency. A narrower sphere than the world never enters His thoughts. He speaks in a natural, spontaneous style, of accomplishing the most arduous and important change in human affairs. This unlabored manner of expressing great thoughts is particularly worthy of attention. You never hear from Jesus that swelling, pompous, ostentatious language, which almost necessarily springs from an attempt to sustain a character above our powers. He talks of His glories as one to whom they were familiar, and of His intimacy and oneness with God as simply as a child speaks of his connection with his parents. He speaks of saving and judging the world, of drawing all men to Himself, and of giving everlasting life, as we speak of the ordinary powers which we exert. He makes no set harangues about the grandeur of His office and character. His consciousness of it gives a hue to His whole language, breaks out in indirect, undesigned expressions, showing that it was the deepest and most familiar of His convictions.

This argument is only to be understood by reading the Gospels with a wakeful mind and heart. It does not lie on their surface, and it is the stronger for lying beneath it. When I read these books with care, when I trace the unaffected majesty which runs through the life of Jesus, and see him never falling below His sublime claims amidst poverty, and scorn, and in His last agony, I have a feeling of the reality of His character which I can not express. I feel that the Jewish carpenter could no more have conceived and sustained this character under motives of imposture than an infant's arm could repeat the deeds of Hercules, or his unawakened intellect comprehend and rival the matchless works of genius.

Am I told that the claims of Jesus had their origin not in imposture, but in enthusiasm; that the imagination, kindled by strong feeling, overpowered the judgment so far as to give Him the notion of being destined to some strange and unparalleled work? I know that enthusiasm, or a kindled imagination, has great power; and we are never to lose sight of it, in judging of the claims of religious teachers. But I say first, that, except in cases where it amounts to insanity, enthusiasm works, in a greater or less degree, according to a man's previous conceptions and modes of thought.

In Judea, where the minds of men were burning with feverish expectation of a messiah, I can easily conceive of a Jew imagining that in himself this ardent conception, this ideal of glory, was to be realized. I can conceive of his seating himself in fancy on the throne of David, and secretly pondering the means of his appointed triumphs. But that a Jew should fancy himself the Messiah, and at the same time should strip that character of all the attributes which had fired his youthful imagination and heart—that he should start aside from all the feelings and hopes of his age, and should acquire a consciousness of being destined to a wholly new career, and one as unbounded as it was now— this is exceedingly improbable; and one thing is certain that an imagination so erratic, so ungoverned, and able to generate the conviction of being destined to work so immeasurably disproportioned to the power of the individual, must have partaken of insanity.

Now, is it conceivable that an individual, mastered by so wild and fervid an imagination, should have sustained the dignity claimed by Christ, should have acted worthily the highest part ever assumed on earth? Would not his enthusiasm have broken out amidst the peculiar excitements of the life of Jesus, and have left a touch of madness on his teaching and conduct? Is it to such a man that we should look for the inculcation of a new and perfect form of virtue, and for the exemplification of humanity in its fairest form?

The charge of an extravagant, self-deluding enthusiasm is the last to be fastened on Jesus. Where can we find the traces of it in His history? Do we detect them in the calm authority of His precepts; in the mild, practical and beneficial spirit of His religion; in the unlabored simplicity of the language with which He unfolds His high powers and the sublime truths of religion; or in the good sense, the knowledge of human nature, which He always discovers in His estimate and treatment of the different classes of men with whom He acted? Do we discover this enthusiasm in the singular fact that, whilst He claimed power in the future world, and always turned men's minds to Heaven, He never indulged His own imagination or stimulated that of His disciples by giving vivid pictures or any minute description of that unseen state?

The truth is, that, remarkable as was the character of Jesus, it was distinguished by nothing more than by calmness and self-possession. This trait pervades His other excellences. How calm was His piety! Point me, if you can, to one vehement, passionate expression of His religious feelings. Does the Lord's Prayer breathe a feverish enthusiasm? The habitual style of Jesus on the subject of religion, if introduced into many churches of His followers at the present day, would be charged with coldness. The calm and the rational character of His piety is particularly seen in the doctrine which He so earnestly inculcates, that disinterested love and self-denying service to our fellow creatures are the most acceptable worship we can offer to our Creator.

His benevolence, too, tho singularly earnest and deep, was composed and serene. He never lost the possession of Himself in His sympathy with others; was never hurried into the impatient and rash enterprises of an enthusiastic philanthropy; but did good with the tranquility and constancy which mark the providence of God. The depth of this calmness may best be understood by considering the opposition made to His claims.

His labors were everywhere insidiously watched and industriously thwarted by vindictive foes who had even conspired to compass, through His death, the ruin of His cause. Now, a feverish enthusiasm which fancies itself to be intrusted with a great work of God is singularly liable to impatient indignation under furious and malignant opposition. Obstacles increase its vehemence; it becomes more eager and hurried in the accomplishment of its purposes, in proportion as they are withstood.

Be it therefore remembered that the malignity of Christ's foes, tho never surpassed, and for the time triumphant, never robbed Him of self-possession, roused no passion, and threw no vehemence or precipitation into His exertions. He did not disguise from Himself or His followers the impression made on the multitude by His adversaries. He distinctly foresaw the violent death towards which He was fast approaching. Yet, confiding in God and in the silent progress of His truth, He possest His soul in peace. Not only was He calm, but His calmness rises into sublimity when we consider the storms which raged around Him and the vastness of the prospects in which His spirit found repose. I say then that serenity and self-possession were peculiarly the attributes of Jesus. I affirm that the singular and sublime character claimed by Jesus can be traced neither to imposture nor to an ungoverned, insane imagination. It can only be accounted for by its truth, its reality.

I began with observing how our long familiarity with Jesus blunts our minds to His singular excellence. We probably have often read of the character which He claimed, without a thought of its extraordinary nature. But I know nothing so sublime. The plans and labors of statesmen sink into the sports of children when compared with the work which Jesus announced, and to which He devoted Himself in life and death with a thorough consciousness of its reality.

The idea of changing the moral aspect of the whole earth, of recovering all nations to the pure and inward worship of one God and to a spirit of divine and fraternal love, was one of which we meet not a trace in philosopher or legislator before Him. The human mind had given no promise of this extent of view. The conception of this enterprise, and the calm, unshaken expectation of success in one who had no station and no wealth, who cast from Him the sword with abhorrence, and who forbade His disciples to use any weapons but those of love, discover a wonderful trust in the power of God and the power of love; and when to this we add that Jesus looked not only to the triumph of His pure faith in the present world, but to a mighty and beneficent power in Heaven, we witness a vastness of purpose, a grandeur of thought and feeling so original, so superior to the workings of all other minds, that nothing but our familiarity can prevent our contemplation of it with wonder and profound awe. * * *

Here is the most striking view of Jesus. This combination of the spirit of humanity, in its lowliest, tenderest form, with the consciousness of unrivaled and divine glories, is the most wonderful distinction of this wonderful character. Here we learn the chief reason why He chose poverty and refused every peculiarity of manner and appearance. He did this because He desired to come near to the multitude of men, to make Himself accessible to all, to pour out the fulness of His sympathy upon all, to know and weep over their sorrows and sins, and to manifest His interest in their affections and joys.

I can offer but a few instances of this sympathy of Christ with human nature in all its varieties of character and condition. But how beautiful are they! At the very opening of His ministry we find Him present at a marriage to which He and His disciples had been called. Among the Jews this was an occasion of peculiar exhilaration and festivity; but Jesus did not therefore decline it. He knew what affections, joys, sorrows, and moral influences are bound up in this institution, and He went to the celebration, not as an ascetic, to frown on its bright hopes and warm congratulations, but to sanction it by His presence and to heighten its enjoyments.

How little does this comport with the solitary dignity which we should have pronounced most accordant with His character, and what a spirit of humanity does it breathe! But this event stands almost alone in His history. His chief sympathy was not with them that rejoice, but with the ignorant, sinful, sorrowful; and with these we find Him cultivating an habitual intimacy. Tho so exalted in thought and purpose, He chose uneducated men to be His chief disciples; and He lived with them, not as a superior, giving occasional and formal instruction, but became their companion traveled with them on foot, slept in their dwellings, sat at their tables, partook of their plain fare, communicated to them His truth in the simplest form; and tho they constantly misunderstood Him and never perceived His full meaning, He was never wearied with teaching them.

So familiar was His intercourse that we find Peter reproving Him with an affectionate zeal for announcing His approaching death, and we find John leaning on His bosom. Of His last discourse to these disciples I need not speak. It stands alone among all writings for the union of tenderness and majesty. His own sorrows are forgotten in His solicitude to speak peace and comfort to His humble followers.

The depth of His human sympathies was beautifully manifested when children were brought Him. His disciples, judging as all men would judge, thought that He was sent to wear the crown of universal empire, had too great a work before Him to give His time and attention to children, and reproved the parents who brought them; but Jesus, rebuking His disciples, called to Him the children. Never, I believe, did childhood awaken such deep love as at that moment. He took them in His arms and blest them, and not only said that "of such was the kingdom of heaven," but added, "He that receiveth a little child in My name, receiveth Me;" so entirely did He identify Himself with this primitive, innocent, beautiful form of human nature.

There was no class of human beings so low as to be beneath His sympathy. He not merely taught the publican and sinner, but, with all His consciousness of purity, sat down and dined with them, and, when reproved by the malignant Pharisee for such companionship, answered by the touching parables of the Lost Sheep and the Prodigal Son, and said, "I am come to seek and to save that which was lost."

No personal suffering dried up this fountain of love in His breast. On His way to the cross He heard some women of Jerusalem bewailing Him, and at the sound, forgetting His own grief, He turned to them and said, "Women of Jerusalem, weep not for Me, but weep for yourselves and your children." On the cross, whilst His mind was divided between intense suffering and the contemplation of the infinite blessings in which His sufferings were to issue, His eye lighted on His mother and John, and the sensibilities of a son and a friend mingled with the sublime consciousness of the universal Lord and Savior. Never before did natural affection find so tender and beautiful an utterance. To His mother He said, directing her to John, "Behold thy son; I leave My beloved disciple to take My place, to perform My filial offices, and to enjoy a share of that affection with which you have followed Me through life;" and to John He said, "Behold thy mother; I bequeath to you the happiness of ministering to My dearest earthly friend." Nor is this all. The spirit of humanity had one higher triumph. Whilst His enemies surrounded Him with a malignity unsoftened by His last agonies, and, to give the keenest edge to insult, reminded Him scoffingly of the high character and office which He had claimed, His only notice of them was the prayer, "Father, forgive them, they know not what they do."

Thus Jesus lived with men; with the consciousness of unutterable majesty He joined a lowliness, gentleness, humanity, and sympathy, which have no example in human history. I ask you to contemplate this wonderful union. In proportion to the superiority of Jesus to all around Him was the intimacy, the brotherly love, with which He bound Himself to them. I maintain that this is a character wholly remote from human conception. To imagine it to be the production of imposture or enthusiasm shows a strange unsoundness of mind. I contemplate it with a veneration second only to the profound awe with which I look up to God. It bears no mark of human invention. It was real. It belonged to and it manifested the beloved Son of God.

But I have not done. May I ask your attention a few moments more? We have not yet reached the depth of Christ's character. We have not touched the great principle on which His wonderful sympathy was founded, and which endeared to Him His office of universal Savior. Do you ask what this deep principle was? I answer, it was His conviction of the greatness of the human soul. He saw in man the impress and image of the Divinity, and therefore thirsted for his redemption, and took the tenderest interest in him, whatever might be the rank, character, or condition in which he was found. This spiritual view of man pervades and distinguishes the teaching of Christ.

Jesus looked on men with an eye which pierced beneath the material frame. The body vanished before Him. The trappings of the rich, the rags of the poor, were nothing to Him. He looked through them, as tho they did not exist, to the soul; and there, amidst clouds of ignorance and plague-spots of sin, He recognized a spiritual and immortal nature, and the germs of power and perfection which might be unfolded forever. In the most fallen and depraved man He saw a being who might become an angel of light.

Still more, He felt that there was nothing in Himself to which men might not ascend. His own lofty consciousness did not sever Him from the multitude; for He saw in His own greatness the model of what men might become. So deeply was He thus imprest that, again and again, in speaking of His future glories, He announced that in these His true followers were to share. They were to sit on His throne and partake of His beneficent power.

Here I pause, and indeed I know not what can be added to heighten the wonder, reverence, and love which are due to Jesus. When I consider Him, not only as possest with the consciousness of an unexampled and unbounded majesty, but as recognizing a kindred nature in human beings, and living and dying to raise them to a participation of His divine glories; and when I see Him under these views allying Himself to men by the tenderest ties, embracing them with a spirit of humanity which no insult, injury, or pain could for a moment repel or overpower, I am filled with wonder as well as reverence and love. I feel that this character is not of human invention, that it was not assumed through fraud, or struck out by enthusiasm; for it is infinitely above their reach. When I add this character of Jesus to the other evidences of His religion, it gives to what before seemed so strange a new and a vast accession of strength; I feel as if I could not be deceived.

The Gospels must be true; they were drawn from a living original; they were founded on reality. The character of Jesus is not a fiction; He was what He claimed to be, and what His followers attested. Nor is this all. Jesus not only was, He is still the Son of God, the Savior of the world. He exists now; He has entered that heaven to which He always looked forward on earth. There He lives and reigns. With a clear, calm faith I see Him in that state of glory; and I confidently expect, at no distant period, to see Him face to face. We have indeed no absent friend whom we shall so surely meet.

Let us then, my hearers, by imitation of His virtues and obedience to His word, prepare ourselves to join Him in those pure mansions where He is surrounding Himself with the good and pure of our race, and will communicate to them forever His own spirit, power, and joy.

CHALMERS

THE EXPULSIVE POWER OF A NEW AFFECTION

BIOGRAPHICAL NOTE

Thomas Chalmers, theologian, preacher and philanthropist, was born at Anstruther, near St. Andrews, Scotland, in 1780. In his thirty-fifth year he experienced a profound religious change and became a pronounced, tho independent, evangelical preacher. On being appointed to the Tron Church in Glasgow, he set about to face what he called "the home heathenism." During the week days he delivered his series of "Astronomical Discourses," in which he endeavored to bring science into harmony with Christianity. His "Commercial Discourses" were designed to Christianize the principles of trade. But he reduced pauperism chiefly by fighting against intemperance in Glasgow. On being transferred to St. John's Parish, the largest, but poorest in the city, he made Edward Irving his assistant. In 1828 he was called to the chair of theology in Edinburgh University.

But it was as a preacher that he exerted most influence by bringing the evangelical message into relations with the science, the culture, the thinking of his age. In doing this he carried his hearers away by the blazing force of his eloquence. Many times in his preaching he was "in an agony of earnestness," and one of his hearers speaks of "that voice, that face, those great, simple, living thoughts, those floods of resistless eloquence, that piercing, shattering voice!" He died in 1847.

CHALMERS

1780-1847
THE EXPULSIVE POWER OF A NEW AFFECTION

*Love not the world, neither the things that are in the world.
If any man love the world, the love of the Father is not in him.*
—1 John ii., 15.

There are two ways in which a practical moralist may attempt
to displace from the human heart its love of the world; either by
a demonstration of the world's vanity, so as that the heart shall
be prevailed upon simply to withdraw its regards from an object
that is not worthy of it; or, by setting forth another object, even
God, as more worthy of its attachment; so as that the heart shall
be prevailed upon, not to resign an old affection which shall
have nothing to succeed it, but to exchange an old affection for
a new one. My purpose is to show, that from the constitution
of our nature, the former method is altogether incompetent and
ineffectual—and that the latter method will alone suffice for the
rescue and recovery of the heart from the wrong affection that
domineers over it. After having accomplished this purpose, I
shall attempt a few practical observations.

Love may be regarded in two different conditions. The first
is when its object is at a distance, and when it becomes love in
a state of desire. The second is when its object is in possession,
and then it becomes love in a state of indulgence. Under the
impulse of desire, man feels himself urged onward in some
path or pursuit of activity for its gratification. The faculties of
his mind are put into busy exercise. In the steady direction of
one great and engrossing interest, his attention is recalled from

51

the many reveries into which it might otherwise have wandered; and the powers of his body are forced away from an indolence in which it else might have languished; and that time is crowded with occupation, which but for some object of keen and devoted ambition, might have driveled along in successive hours of weariness and distaste—and tho hope does not always enliven, and success does not always crown the career of exertion, yet in the midst of this very variety, and with the alternations of occasional disappointment, is the machinery of the whole man kept in a sort of congenial play, and upholden in that tone and temper which are most agreeable to it; insomuch that, if through the extirpation of that desire which forms the originating principle of all this movement, the machinery were to stop, and to receive no impulse from another desire substituted in its place, the man would be leftwith all his propensities to action in a state of most painful and unnatural abandonment. A sensitive being suffers, and is in violence, if, after having thoroughly rested from his fatigue, or been relieved from his pain, he continue in possession of powers without any excitement to these powers; if he possess a capacity of desire without having an object of desire; or if he have a spare energy upon his person, without a counterpart, and without a stimulus to call it into operation. The misery of such a condition is often realized by him who is retired from business, or who is retired from law, or who is even retired from the occupations of the chase, and of the gaming-table. Such is the demand of our nature for an object in pursuit, that no accumulation of previous success can extinguish it—and thus it is, that the most prosperous merchant, and the most victorious general, and the most fortunate gamester, when the labor of their respective vocations has come to a close, are often found to languish in the midst of all their acquisitions, as if out of their kindred and rejoicing element. It is quite in vain, with such a constitutional appetite for employment in man, to attempt cutting away from him the spring or the principle of one employment, without providing him with another. The whole heart and habit will rise in resistance against such an undertaking. The else unoccupied female, who spends the hours of every evening at some play of hazard, knows as well as you, that the pecuniary gain, or the honorable triumph of a successful contest, are altogether paltry. It is not such a demonstration of vanity as this that will force her away from her dear and delightful occupation. The habit can not so be displaced as to leave nothing but a negative and cheerless vacancy behind it—tho it may be so supplanted as to be followed up by another habit of employment, to which the power of some new affection has constrained her. It is willingly suspended, for example, on any single evening, should the time that is wont to be allotted to gaming be required to be spent on the preparations of an approaching assembly.

The ascendant power of a second affection will do what no exposition, however forcible, of the folly and worthlessness of the first, ever could effectuate. And it is the same in the great world. You never will be able to arrest any of its leading pursuits by a naked demonstration of their vanity. It is quite in vain to think of stopping one of these pursuits in any way else but by stimulating to another. In attempting to bring a worthy man, intent and busied with the prosecution of his objects, to a dead stand, you have not merely to encounter the charm which he annexes to these objects, but you have to encounter the pleasure which he feels in the very prosecution of them. It is not enough, then, that you dissipate the charm by your moral and eloquent and affecting exposure of its illusiveness. You must address to the eye of his mind another object, with a charm powerful enough to dispossess the first of its influence, and to engage him in some other prosecution as full of interest and hope and congenial activity as the former. It is this which stamps an impotency on all moral and pathetic declamation about the insignificance of the world. A man will no more consent to the misery of being without an object, because that object is a trifle, or of being without a pursuit, because that pursuit terminates in some frivolous or fugitive acquirement, than he will voluntarily submit himself to the torture, because that torture is to be of short duration. If to be without desire and without exertion altogether is a state of violence and discomfort, then the present desire, with its correspondent train of exertion, is not to be got rid of simply by destroying it. It must be by substituting another desire, and another line or habit of exertion in its place, and the most effectual way of withdrawing the mind from one object is not by turning it away upon desolate and unpeopled vacancy, but by presenting to its regards another object still more alluring.

These remarks apply not merely to love considered in its state of desire for an object not yet obtained. They apply also to love considered in its state of indulgence, or placid gratification, with an object already in possession. It is seldom that any of our tastes are made to disappear by a mere process of natural extinction. At least, it is very seldom that this is done through the instrumentality of reasoning. It may be done by excessive pampering, but it is almost never done by the mere force of mental determination. But what can not be thus destroyed, may be dispossest—and one taste may be made to give way to another, and to lose its power entirely as the reigning affection of the mind. It is thus that the boy ceases, at length, to be the slave of his appetite; but it is because a manlier taste has now brought it into subordination, and that the youth ceases to idolize pleasure; but it is because the idol of wealth has become the stronger and gotten the ascendency, and that even the love of money ceases to have the mastery over the heart of many a thriving citizen; but it is because, drawn into the whirl of city politics, another affection has been wrought into his moral system, and he is now lorded over by the love of power. There is not one of these transformations in which the heart is left without an object. Its desire for one particular object may be conquered; but as to its desire for having some one object or other, this is unconquerable. Its adhesion to that on which it has fastened the preference of its regards, can not willingly be overcome by the rending away of a simple separation. It can be done only by the application of something else, to which it may feel the adhesion of a still stronger and more powerful preference. Such is the grasping tendency of the human heart, that it must have a something to lay hold of—and which, if wrested away without the substitution of another something in its place, would leave a void and a vacancy as painful to the mind as hunger is to the natural system. It may be dispossest of one object, or of any, but it can not be desolated of all. Let there be a breathing and a sensitive heart, but without a liking and without affinity to any of the things that are around it, and in a state of cheerless abandonment, it would be alive to nothing but the burden of its own consciousness, and feel it to be intolerable. It would make no difference to its owner, whether he dwelt in the midst of a gay and a goodly world, or, placed afar beyond the outskirts of creation, he dwelt a solitary unit in dark and unpeopled nothingness. The heart must have something to cling to—and never, by its own voluntary consent, will it so denude itself of all its attachments that there shall not be one remaining object that can draw or solicit it.

The misery of a heart thus bereft of all relish for that which is wont to minister enjoyment, is strikingly exemplified in those who, satiated with indulgence, have been so belabored, as it were, with the variety and the poignancy of the pleasurable sensations that they have experienced, that they are at length fatigued out of all capacity for sensation whatever. The disease of ennui is more frequent in the French metropolis, where amusement is more exclusively the occupation of higher classes, than it is in the British metropolis, where the longings of the heart are more diversified by the resources of business and politics. There are the votaries of fashion, who, in this way, have at length become the victims of fashionable excess; in whom the very multitude of their enjoyments has at last extinguished their power of enjoyment; who, with the gratifications of art and nature at command, now look upon all that is around them with an eye of tastelessness; who, plied with the delights of sense and of splendor even to weariness, and incapable of higher delights, have come to the end of all their perfection, and, like Solomon of old, found it to be vanity and vexation. The man whose heart has thus been turned into a desert can vouch for the insupportable languor which must ensue, when one affection is thus plucked away from the bosom, without another to replace it. It is not necessary that a man receive pain from anything, in order to become miserable. It is barely enough that he looks with distaste to everything, and in that asylum which is the repository of minds out of joint, and where the organ of feeling as well as the organ of intellect has been impaired, it is not in the cell of loud and frantic outcries where you will meet with the acme of mental suffering; but that is the individual who outpeers in wretchedness all his fellows, who throughout the whole expanse of nature and society meets not an object that has at all the power to detain or to interest him; who neither in earth beneath, nor in heaven above, knows of a single charm to which his heart can send forth one desirous or responding movement; to whom the world, in his eye a vast and empty desolation, has left him nothing but his own consciousness to feed upon, dead to all that is without him, and alive to nothing but to the load of his own torpid and useless existence.

We know not a more sweeping interdict upon the affections of nature, than that which is delivered by the apostle in the verse before us. To bid a man into whom there is not yet entered the great and ascendant influence of the principle of regeneration, to bid him withdraw his love from all the things that are in the world, is to bid him give up all the affections that are in his heart. The world is the all of a natural man. He has not a taste, nor a desire, that points not to a something placed within the confines of its visible horizon. He loves nothing above it, and he cares for nothing beyond it; and to bid him love not the world is to pass a sentence of expulsion on all the inmates of his bosom. To estimate the magnitude and the difficulty of such a surrender, let us only think that it were just as arduous to prevail on him not to love wealth, which is but one of the things in the world, as to prevail on him to set wilful fire to his own property. This he might do with sore and painful reluctance, if he saw that the salvation of his life hung upon it. But this he would do willingly if he saw that a new property of tenfold value was instantly to emerge from the wreck of the old one. In this case there is something more than the mere displacement of an affection. There is the overbearing of one affection by another. But to desolate his heart of all love for the things of the world without the substitution of any love in its place, were to him a process of as unnatural violence as to destroy all the things he has in the world, and give him nothing in their room. So if to love not the world be indispensable to one's Christianity, then the crucifixion of the old man is not too strong a term to mark that transition in his history, when all old things are done away, and all things are become new.

The love of the world can not be expunged by a mere demonstration of the world's worthlessness. But may it not be supplanted by the love of that which is more worthy than itself? The heart can not be prevailed upon to part with the world, by a simple act of resignation. But may not the heart be prevailed upon to admit into its preference another, who shall subordinate the world, and bring it down from its wonted ascendency? If the throne which is placed there must have an occupier, and the tyrant that now reigns has occupied it wrongfully, he may not leave a bosom which would rather detain him than be left in desolation. But may he not give way to the lawful Sovereign, appearing with every charm that can secure His willing admittance, and taking unto Himself His great power to subdue the moral nature of man, and to reign over it? In a word, if the way to disengage the heart from the positive love of one great and ascendant object is to fasten it in positive love to another, then it is not by exposing the worthlessness of the former, but by addressing to the mental eye the worth and excellence of the latter, that all old things are to be done away, and all things are to become new.

This, we trust, will explain the operation of that charm which accompanies the effectual preaching of the gospel. The love of God, and the love of the world, are two affections, not merely in a state of rivalship, but in a state of enmity, and that so irreconcilable that they can not dwell together in the same bosom. We have already affirmed how impossible it were for the heart, by any innate elasticity of its own, to cast the world away from it, and thus reduce itself to a wilderness. The heart is not so constituted, and the only way to dispossess it of an old affection is by the expulsive power of a new one. Nothing can exceed the magnitude of the required change in a man's character—when bidden, as he is in the New Testament, to love not the world; no, nor any of the things that are in the world—for this so comprehends all that is dear to him in existence as to be equivalent to a command of self-annihilation. But the same revelation which dictates so mighty an obedience places within our reach as mighty an instrument of obedience. It brings for admittance, to the very door of our heart, an affection which, once seated upon its throne, will either subordinate every previous inmate, or bid it away. Beside the world it places before the eye of the mind Him who made the world, and with this peculiarity, which is all its own—that in the gospel do we so behold God as that we may love God. It is there, and there only, where God stands revealed as an object of confidence to sinners—and where our desire after Him is not chilled into apathy by that barrier of human guilt which intercepts every approach that is not made to Him through the appointed Mediator. It is the bringing in of this better hope, whereby we draw nigh unto God—and to live without hope is to live without God, and if the heart be without God the world will then have all the ascendency. It is God apprehended by the believer as God in Christ who alone can dispost it from this ascendency. It is when He stands dismantled of the terrors which belong to Him as an offended lawgiver, and when we are enabled by faith, which is His own gift, to see His glory in the face of Jesus Christ, and to hear His beseeching voice, as it protests good-will to men, and entreats the return of all who will to a full pardon, and a gracious acceptance—it is then that a love paramount to the love of the world, and at length expulsive of it, first arises in the regenerating bosom. It is when released from the spirit of bondage, with which love can not dwell, and when admitted into the number of God's children, through the faith that is in Christ Jesus, the spirit of adoption is poured upon us—it is then that the heart, brought under the mastery of one great and predominant affection, is delivered from the tyranny of its former desires, and in the only way in which deliverance is possible. And that faith which is revealed to us from heaven, as indispensable to a sinner's justification in the sight of God, is also the instrument of the greatest of all moral and spiritual achievements on a nature dead to the influence, and beyond the reach of every other application.

Let us not cease then to ply the only instrument of powerful and positive operation, to do away from you the love of the world. Let us try every legitimate method of finding access to your hearts for the love of Him who is greater than the world. For this purpose let us, if possible, clear away that shroud of unbelief which so hides and darkens the face of Deity. Let us insist on His claims to your affection; and whether in the shape of gratitude, or in the shape of esteem, let us never cease to affirm that in the whole of that wondrous economy, the purpose of which is to reclaim a sinful world unto Himself, He, the God of love, so sets Himself forth in characters of endearment that naught but faith, and naught but understanding are wanting, on your part, to call forth the love of your hearts back again.

And here let me advert to the incredulity of a worldly man when he brings his own sound and secular experience to bear upon the high doctrines of Christianity, when he looks on regeneration as a thing impossible, when, feeling, as he does, the obstinacies of his own heart on the side of things present, and casting an intelligent eye, much exercised perhaps in the observation of human life, on the equal obstinacies of all who are around him, he pronounces this whole matter about the crucifixion of the old man, and the resurrection of a new man in his place, to be in downright opposition to all that is known and witnessed of the real nature of humanity. We think that we have seen such men, who, firmly trenched in their own vigorous and home-bred sagacity, and shrewdly regardful of all that passes before them through the week, and upon the scenes of ordinary business, look on that transition of the heart by which it gradually dies unto time, and awakens in all the life of a new-felt and ever-growing desire toward God, as a mere Sabbath speculation; and who thus, with all their attention engrossed upon the concerns of earthliness, continue unmoved, to the end of their days, among the feelings, and the appetites, and the pursuits of earthliness. If the thought of death, and another state of being after it, comes across them at all, it is not with a change so radical as that of being born again that they ever connect the idea of preparation. They have some vague conception of its being quite enough that they acquit themselves in some decent and tolerable way of their relative obligations; and that, upon the strength of some such social and domestic moralities as are often realized by him in whose heart the love of God has never entered, they will be transplanted in safety from this world, where God is the Being with whom, it may almost be said that, they have had nothing to do, to that world where God is the Being with whom they will have mainly and immediately to do throughout all eternity. They will admit all that is said of the utter vanity of time, when taken up with as a resting-place. But they resist every application made upon the heart of man, with the view of so shifting its tendencies that it shall not henceforth find in the interests of time all its rest and all its refreshment. They, in fact, regard such an attempt as an enterprise that is altogether aerial—and with a tone of secular wisdom, caught from the familiarities of every day of experience, do they see a visionary character in all that is said of setting our affections on the things that are above; and of walking by faith; and of keeping our hearts in such a love of God as shall shut out from them the love of the world; and of having no confidence in the flesh; and of so renouncing earthly things as to have our conversation in heaven.

Now, it is altogether worthy of being remarked of those men who thus disrelish spiritual Christianity, and, in fact, deem it an impracticable acquirement, how much of a piece their incredulity about the demands of Christianity, and their incredulity about the doctrines of Christianity, are with one another. No wonder that they feel the work of the New Testament to be beyond their strength, so long as they hold the words of the New Testament to be beneath their attention. Neither they nor anyone else can dispossess the heart of an old affection, but by the impulsive power of a new one—and, if that new affection be the love of God, neither they nor anyone else can be made to entertain it, but on such a representation of the Deity as shall draw the heart of the sinner toward Him. Now it is just their belief which screens from the discernment of their minds this representation. They do not see the love of God in sending His Son into the world. They do not see the expression of His tenderness to men, in sparing Him not, but giving Him up unto the death for us all. They do not see the sufficiency of the atonement, or of the sufferings that were endured by Him who bore the burden that sinners should have borne. They do not see the blended holiness and compassion of the Godhead, in that He passed by the transgressions of His creatures, yet could not pass them by without an expiation. It is a mystery to them how a man should pass to the state of godliness from a state of nature—but had they only a believing view of God manifest in the flesh, this would resolve for them the whole mystery of godliness. As it is, they can not get quit of their old affections, because they are out of sight from all those truths which have influence to raise a new one. They are like the children of Israel in the land of Egypt, when required to make bricks without straw they cannot love God, while they want the only food which can aliment this affection in a sinner's bosom—and however great their errors may be, both in resisting the demands of the gospel as impracticable, and in rejecting the doctrines of the gospel as inadmissible, yet there is not a spiritual man (and it is the prerogative of him who is spiritual to judge all men) who will not perceive that there is a consistency in these errors.

But if there be a consistency in the errors, in like manner, is there a consistency in the truths which are opposite to them? The man who believes in the peculiar doctrines will readily bow to the peculiar demands of Christianity. When he is told to love God supremely, this may startle another, but it will not startle him to whom God has been revealed in peace, and in pardon, and in all the freeness of an offered reconciliation. When told to shut out the world from his heart, this may be impossible with him who has nothing to replace it—but not impossible with him who has found in God a sure and satisfying portion. When told to withdraw his affections from the things that are beneath, this were laying an order of self-extinction upon the man, who knows not another quarter in the whole sphere of his contemplation to which he could transfer them, but it were not grievous to him whose view had been opened to the loveliness and glory of the things that are above, and can there find, for every feeling of his soul, a most ample and delighted occupation. When told to look not to the things that are seen and temporal, this were blotting out the light of all that is visible from the prospect of him in whose eye there is a wall of partition between guilty nature and the joys of eternity—but he who believes that Christ has broken down this wall finds a gathering radiance upon his soul, as he looks onward in faith to the things that are unseen and eternal. Tell a man to be holy—and how can he compass such a performance, when his fellowship with holiness is a fellowship of despair? It is the atonement of the cross reconciling the holiness of the lawgiver with the safety of the offender, that hath opened the way for a sanctifying influence into the sinner's heart, and he can take a kindred impression from the character of God now brought nigh, and now at peace with him. Separate the demand from the doctrine, and you have either a system of righteousness that is impracticable, or a barren orthodoxy. Bring the demand and the doctrine together, and the true disciple of Christ is able to do the one, through the other strengthening him. The motive is adequate to the movement; and the bidden obedience to the gospel is not beyond the measure of his strength, just because the doctrine of the gospel is not beyond the measure of his acceptance. The shield of faith, and the hope of salvation, and the Word of God, and the girdle of truth, these are the armor that he has put on; and with these the battle is won, and the eminence is reached, and the man stands on the vantage ground of a new field and a new prospect. The effect is great, but the cause is equal to it, and stupendous as this moral resurrection to the precepts of Christianity undoubtedly is, there is an element of strength enough to give it being and continuance in the principles of Christianity.

The object of the gospel is both to pacify the sinner's conscience and to purify his heart; and it is of importance to observe, that what mars the one of these objects mars the other also. The best way of casting out an impure affection is to admit a pure one; and by the love of what is good to expel the love of what is evil. Thus it is, that the freer gospel, the more sanctifying is the gospel; and the more it is received as a doctrine of grace, the more will it be felt as a doctrine according to godliness. This is one of the secrets of the Christian life, that the more a man holds of God as a pensioner, the greater is the payment of service that He renders back again. On the venture of "Do this and live," a spirit of fearfulness is sure to enter; and the jealousies of a legal bargain chase away all confidence from the intercourse between God and man; and the creature striving to be square and even with his creator is, in fact, pursuing all the while his own selfishness instead of God's glory; and with all the conformities which he labors to accomplish, the soul of obedience is not there, the mind is not subject to the law of God, nor indeed under such an economy ever can be. It is only when, as in the gospel, acceptance is bestowed as a present, without money and without price, that the security which man feels in God is placed beyond the reach of disturbance, or that he can repose in Him as one friend reposes in another; or that any liberal and generous understanding can be established betwixt them, the one party rejoicing over the other to do him good, the other finding that the truest gladness of his heart lies in the impulse of a gratitude by which it is awakened to the charms of a new moral existence. Salvation by grace—salvation by free grace—salvation not of works, but according to the mercy of God, salvation on such a footing is not more indispensable to the deliverance of our persons from the hand of justice than it is to the deliverance of our hearts from the chill and the weight of ungodliness. Retain a single shred or fragment of legality with the gospel, and you raise a topic of distrust between man and God. You take away from the power of the gospel to melt and to conciliate. For this purpose the freer it is the better it is. That very peculiarity which so many dread as the germ of Antinomianism, is, in fact, the germ of a new spirit and a new inclination against it. Along with the lights of a free gospel does there enter the love of the gospel, which, in proportion as you impair the freeness, you are sure to chase away. And never does the sinner find within himself so mighty a moral transformation as when, under the belief that he is saved by grace, he feels constrained thereby to offer his heart a devoted thing, and to deny ungodliness.

To do any work in the best manner, you would make use of the fittest tools for it. And we trust that what has been said may serve in some degree for the practical guidance of those who would like to reach the great moral achievement of our text, but feel that the tendencies and desires of nature are too strong for them. We know of no other way by which to keep the love of the world out of our heart than to keep in our hearts the love of God—and no other way by which to keep our hearts in the love of God, than by building ourselves on our most holy faith. That denial of the world which is not possible to him that dissents from the gospel testimony, is possible, even as all things are possible, to him that believeth. To try this without faith is to work without the right tool or the right instrument. But faith worketh by love; and the way of expelling from the heart the love that transgresseth the law is to admit into its receptacles the love which fulfilleth the law.

Conceive a man to be standing on the margin of this green world, and that, when he looked toward it, he saw abundance smiling upon every field, and all the blessings which earth can afford scattered in profusion throughout every family, and the light of the sun sweetly resting upon all the pleasant habitations, and the joys of human companionship brightening many a happy circle of society; conceive this to be the general character of the scene upon one side of his contemplation, and that on the other, beyond the verge of the goodly planet on which he was situated, he could descry nothing but a dark and fathomless unknown. Think you that he would bid a voluntary adieu to all the brightness and all the beauty that were before him upon earth, and commit himself to the frightful solitude away from it? Would he leave its peopled dwelling places, and become a solitary wanderer through the fields of nonentity? If space offered him nothing but a wilderness, would he for it abandon the home-bred scenes of life and cheerfulness that lay so near, and exerted such a power of urgency to detain him? Would not he cling to the regions of sense, and of life, and of society? Shrinking away from the desolation that was beyond it, would not he be glad to keep his firm footing on the territory of this world, and to take shelter under the silver canopy that was stretched over it?

But if, during the time of his contemplation, some happy island of the blest had floated by, and there had burst upon his senses the light of surpassing glories, and its sounds of sweeter melody, and he clearly saw there a purer beauty rested upon every field, and a more heartfelt joy spread itself among all the families, and he could discern there a peace, and a piety, and a benevolence which put a moral gladness into every bosom, and united the whole society in one rejoicing sympathy with each other, and with the beneficent Father of them all. Could he further see that pain and mortality were there unknown, and above all, that signals of welcome were hung out, and an avenue of communication was made before him—perceive you not that what was before the wilderness, would become the land of invitation, and that now the world would be the wilderness? What unpeopled space could not do, can be done by space teeming with beatific scenes, and beatific society. And let the existing tendencies of the heart be what they may to the scene that is near and visible around us, still if another stood revealed to the prospect of man, either through the channel of faith or through the channel of his senses—then, without violence done to the constitution of his moral nature, may he die unto the present world, and live to the lovelier world that stands in the distance away from it.

CAMPBELL

THE MISSIONARY CAUSE

BIOGRAPHICAL NOTE

Alexander Campbell, prominent in the body known as Disciples or Christians, was born in Ireland in 1788, and received his education in Glasgow University. In 1809 he emigrated to the United States and took charge of a Presbyterian congregation in Bethany, Va. He did not long remain in this pastorate, but proceeded to institute a society based upon the abolition of all confessions and formularies and the acknowledgment of the text of the Holy Scriptures as the sole creed of the Church. In 1841 he founded Bethany College (Bethany, Va.), and remained its president until his death in 1866. In 1823 he founded the *Christian Baptist*, changed its name in 1829 to the *Millennial Harbinger*, but abandoned it three years before his death. He was a prolific controversial writer and published over fifty volumes, among which were hymn books and a translation of the New Testament.

CAMPBELL

1788-1866
THE MISSIONARY CAUSE[1]

He that winneth souls is wise.—Prov. xi., 30.

The missionary cause is older than the material universe. It was celebrated by Job—the oldest poet on the pages of time.

Jehovah challenges Job to answer Him a few questions on the institutions of the universe. "Gird up now thy loins," said He; "and I will demand of thee a few responses. Where wast thou when I laid the foundations of the earth? Declare, if thou hast understanding. Who has fixt the measure thereof? Or who has stretched the line upon it? What are the foundations thereof? Who has laid the corner-stone thereof when the morning stars sang together, and all the sons of God shouted for joy? Who shut up the sea with doors when it burst forth issuing from the womb of eternity—when I made a cloud its garment, and thick darkness its swaddling band? I appointed its limits, saying, Thus far shalt thou come, but no farther; and here shall the pride of thy waves be stayed.

"Has the rain a father? Who has begotten the drops of the dew? Who was the mother of the ice? And the hoar-frost of heaven, who has begotten it? Can mortal man bind the bands of the Seven Stars, or loose the cords of Orion? Can he bring forth and commission the twelve signs of the Zodiac, or bind Arcturus with his seven sons?

---

1 Delivered to the American Christian Missionary Society, Cincinnati, October, 1860.

"Knowest thou, oh man, the missionaries of the starry heavens? Canst thou lift up thy voice to the clouds, that abundance of waters may cover thee? Canst thou command the lightnings, so that they may say to thee, Here we are? Who can number the clouds in wisdom? Or who can pour out the bottles of heaven upon the thirsty fields?"

If such be a single page in the volume of God's physical missionaries, what must be its contents could we, by the telescope of an angel, survey one single province of the universe, of universes, which occupy topless, bottomless, boundless space!

We have data in the Bible, and, in the phenomena of the material universe, sufficient to authorize the assumption that the missionary idea circumscribes and permeates the entire area of creations.

Need we inquire into the meaning of a celestial title given to the tenantries of the heaven of heavens? But you all, my Christian brethren, know it. You anticipate me. The sweet poet of Israel told you long since, in his sixty-eighth ode, that the chariots of God are about twenty thousand of angels.[2]

And what is an angel but a messenger, a missionary? Hence the seven angels of the seven churches in Asia were seven missionaries, or messengers, sent to John in his exile; and by these John wrote letters to the seven congregations in Asia.

Figuratively, God makes the winds and lightnings his angels, his messengers of wrath or of mercy, as the case may be.

But we are a missionary society—a society assembled from all points of the compass, assembled, too, we hope, in the true missionary spirit, which is the spirit of Christianity in its primordial conception. God Himself instituted it. Moses is the oldest missionary whose name is inscribed on the rolls of time.

---

2   This is an exact literal version of Rebotayim alphey shenan. The Targum says, "The chariots of God are two myriads—and two thousand angels draw them." A myriad is 10,000—two myriads 20,000. "To know this," Adam Clarke says, "we must die."

He was the first divine missionary, and, if we except John the Baptist, he was the second in rank and character to the Lord Messiah Himself.

Angels and missionaries are rudimentally but two names for the same officers. But of the incarnate Word, God's only begotten Son, He says, "Thou art my son, the beloved, in whom I delight." And He commands the world of humanity to hearken to Him. He was, indeed, God's own special ambassador, invested with all power in heaven and on earth—a true, a real, an everlasting plenipotentiary, having vested in Him all the rights of God and all the rights of man. And were not all the angels of heaven placed under Him as His missionaries, sent forth to minister to the heirs of salvation?

His commission, given to the twelve apostles, is a splendid and glorious commission. Its preamble is wholly unprecedented—"All authority in heaven and on earth is given to me." In pursuance thereof, he gave commission to His apostles, saying, "Go, convert all the nations, immersing them into the name of the Father, and of the Son, and of the Holy Spirit; teaching them to observe all things whatever I have commanded you; and, lo, I am with you always, even to the end of the world." Angels, apostles and evangelists were placed under this command, and by Him commissioned as His ambassadors to the world.

The missionary institution, we repeat, is older than Adam—older than our earth. It is coeval with the origin of angels.

Satan had been expelled from heaven before Adam was created. His assault upon our mother Eve, by an incarnation in the most subtle animal in Paradise, is positive proof of the intensity of his malignity to God and to man. He, too, has his missionaries in the whole area of humanity. Michael and his angels, or missionaries, are, and long have been, in conflict against the devil and his missionaries. The battle, in this our planet, is yet in progress, and therefore missionaries are in perpetual demand. Hence the necessity incumbent on us to carry on this warfare as loyal subjects of the Hero of our redemption.

The Christian armory is well supplied with all the weapons essential to the conflict. We need them all. "We wrestle not against flesh and blood, but against principalities, against powers, against the rulers of the darkness of this world, against wicked spirits in the regions of the air." Hence the need of having our "loins girded with the truth"; having on the breastplate of righteousness, our feet shod with the preparation to publish the gospel of peace, taking the shield of faith, the helmet of salvation and the sword of the Spirit, the Word of God, always praying and making supplication for our fellow-missionaries and for all saints.

The missionary fields are numerous and various. They are both domestic and foreign. The harvest is great in both. The laborers are still few, comparatively very few, in either of them.

The supply is not a tithe of the demand. The Macedonians cry, "Come over and help us;" "Send us an evangelist;" "Send us missionaries;" "The fields are large, the people are desirous, anxious, to hear the original gospel. What can you do for us?" Nothing! Nothing! My brethren, ought this so to be?

Schools for the prophets are wanting. But there is a too general apathy or indifference on the subject. We pray to the Lord of the harvest to send our reapers to gather it into His garner. But what do we besides praying for it? Do we work for it? Suppose a farmer should pray to the Lord for an abundant harvest next year, and should never, in seed-time, turn over one furrow or scatter one handful of seed: what would we think of him? Would not his neighbors regard him as a monomaniac or a simpleton? And wherein does he excel such a one in wisdom or in prudence who prays to the Lord to send out reapers—missionaries, or evangelists—to gather a harvest of souls, when he himself never gives a dollar to a missionary, or the value of it, to enable him to go into the field? Can such a person be in earnest, or have one sincere desire in his heart to effect such an object or purpose? We must confess that we could have no faith either in his head or in his heart.

The heavenly missionaries require neither gold nor silver, neither food nor raiment. Not so the earthly missionaries. They themselves, their wives and children, demand both food and clothing, to say nothing of houses and furniture. Their present home is not

> "The gorgeous city, garnish'd like a bride,Where Christ for spouse expected is to pass,The walls of jasper compass'd on each side,And streets all paved with gold, more bright than glass."

If such were the missionary's home on earth, he might, indeed, labor gratuitously all the days of his life. In an humble cottage— rather an unsightly cabin—we sometimes see the wife of his youth, in garments quite as unsightly as those of her children, impatiently waiting "their sire's return, to climb to his knees the envied kiss to share." But, when the supper table is spread, what a beggarly account of almost empty plates and dishes! Whose soul would not sicken at such a sight? I have twice, if not thrice, in days gone by, when travelling on my early missionary tours— over not the poorest lands nor the poorest settlements, either— witnessed some such cases, and heard of more.

I was then my own missionary, with the consent, however, of one church. I desired to mingle with all classes of religious society, that I might personally and truthfully know, not the theories, but the facts and the actualities, of the Christian ministry and the so-called Christian public. I spent a considerable portion of my time during the years 1812, '13, '14, '15, '16, traveling throughout western Virginia, Pennsylvania, and Ohio.

I then spent seven years in reviewing my past studies, and in teaching the languages and the sciences—after which I extended my evangelical labors into other States and communities, that I might still more satisfactorily apprehend and appreciate the *status*, or the actual condition, of the nominally and profest religious or Christian world.

Having shortly after my baptism connected myself with the Baptist people, and attending their associations as often as I could, I became more and more penetrated with the conviction that theory had usurped the place of faith, and that consequently, human institutions had been, more or less, substituted for the apostolic and the divine.

During this period of investigation I had the pleasure of forming an intimate acquaintance with sundry Baptist ministers, East and West, as well as with the ministry of other denominations. Flattering prospects of usefulness on all sides began to expand before me and to inspire me with the hope of achieving a long-cherished object—doing some good in the advocacy of the primitive and apostolic gospel—having in the year 1820 a discussion on the subject of the first positive institution enacted by the Lord Messiah, and in A. D. 1823 another on the same subject—the former more especially on the subject and action of Christian baptism, the latter more emphatically on the design of that institution tho including the former two.

These discussions, more or less, embraced the rudimental elements of the Christian institution, and gave to the public a bold relief outline of the whole genius, spirit, letter and doctrine of the gospel.

Its missionary spirit, tho not formally propounded, was yet indicated, in these discussions; because this institution was the terminus of the missionary work. It was a component element of the gospel, as clearly seen in the commission of the enthroned Messiah. Its preamble is the superlative fact of the whole Bible. We regret, indeed, that this most sublime preamble has been so much lost sight of even by the present living generation. If we ask when the Church of Jesus Christ began or when the reign of the Heavens commenced, the answer, in what is usually called Christendom, will make it either to be contemporaneous with the ministry of John the Harbinger, or with the birth of the Lord Jesus Christ. We will find one of these two opinions almost universally entertained. The Baptists are generally much attached

74

to John the Baptist; the Pedobaptists, to the commencement of Christ's public ministry. John the Baptist was the first Christian missionary with a very considerable class of living Baptists; the birth of Christ is the most popular and orthodox theory at the respective meridians of Lutheranism, Calvinism, and Arminianism.

But, by the more intelligent, the resurrection, or the ascension of the Lord Jesus Christ, is generally regarded as the definite commencement of the Christian age or institution.

Give us Paul's or Peter's testimony, against that of all theologians, living or dead. Let us look at the facts.

Did not the Savior teach His personal pupils, or disciples, to pray, "Thy kingdom"—more truthfully, "Thy reign—come"? Does any king's reign or kingdom commence with his birth? Still less with his death? Did not our Savior Himself, in person, decline the honors of a worldly or temporal prince? Did He not declare that His kingdom "is not of this world"? Did He not say that He was going hence, or leaving this world, to receive or obtain a kingdom? And were not the keys of the kingdom first given to Peter to open, to announce it? And did he not, when in Jerusalem, on the first Pentecost, after the ascension of the Lord Jesus, make a public proclamation, saying, "Let all the house of Israel know assuredly that God has made (or constituted) the identical Jesus of Nazareth, the son of Mary, both the Lord and the Christ, or the anointed Lord"?

Do kings reign before they are crowned? Before they are anointed? There was not a Christian Church on earth, or any man called a Christian, until after the consecration and coronation of Jesus of Nazareth as the Christ of God.

The era of a son's birth was never, since the world began, the era of his reign or of the commencement of it. It is a strange fact, to me a wonderful fact, and, considering the age in which we live, an overwhelming fact, that we, as a community, are the only people on the checkered map of all Christendom, Greek, Roman, Anglican or American, that preach and teach that the commonly called Christian era is not the era or the commencement of the Christian Church or kingdom of the Lord Jesus the Christ.

The kingdom of the Christ could not antedate His coronation. Hence Peter, in announcing His coronation, after His ascension, proclaimed, saying, "Let all the house of Israel know assuredly that God has made—*touton ton Ieesoun*—the same, the identical Jesus whom you have crucified, both Lord and Christ"; or, in other words, has crowned Him the legitimate Lord of all. Then indeed His reign began. Then was verified the oracle uttered by the royal bard of Israel, "Jehovah said to my Jehovah"—or, "the Lord said to my Lord,"—"Sit thou on my right hand till I make thy foes thy footstool."

Hence He could say, and did say, to His apostles, "All authority in the heavens and on the earth is given to me." In pursuance thereof, "Go you into all the world, proclaim the gospel to the whole creation; assuring them that everyone who believes this proclamation and is immersed into the name of the Father, and of the Son, and of the Holy Spirit, shall be saved."

Here, then, the missionary field is declared to be the whole world—the broad earth. They were, as we are afterwards informed, to begin at the first capital in the land of Judea, then to proceed to Samaria, the capital of the ten tribes, and thence to the last domicile of man on earth.

There was, and there is still, in all this arrangement, a gracious and a glorious propriety.

The Jews had murdered the Messiah under the false charge of an impostor. Was it not, then, divinely grand and supremely glorious to make this awfully bloodstained capital the beginning, the fountain, of the gospel age and mission? Hence it was decreed that all the earth should be the parish, and all the nations and languages of earth the objects, and millions of them the subjects, of the redeeming grace and tender mercies of our Savior and our God.

What an extended and still extending area is the missionary field! There are the four mighty realms of Pagandom, of Papaldom, of Mohammedandom and of ecclesiastic Sectariandom. These are, one and all, essentially and constitutionally, more or less, not of the apostolic Christendom.

The divinely inspired constitution of the Church contains only seven articles. These are the seven hills, not of Rome, but of the true Zion of Israel's God. Paul's summary of them is found in the following words: "One body, one spirit, one hope, one Lord, one faith, one baptism, and one God and Father of all."

The clear perception, the grateful reception, the cordial entertainment of these seven divinely constructed and instituted pillars, are the alone sufficient, and the all-sufficient, foundation—the indestructible basis—of Christ's kingdom on this earth, and of man's spiritual and eternal salvation in the full enjoyment of himself, his Creator, his Redeemer, and the whole universe of spiritual intelligence through all the circles and the cycles of an infinite, an everlasting future of being and of blessedness.

The missionary spirit is, indeed, an emanation of the whole Godhead. God the Father sent His Son, His only begotten Son, into our world. The Son sent the Holy Spirit to bear witness through His twelve missionaries, the consecrated and Heaven-inspired apostles. They proclaimed the glad tidings of great joy to all people—to the Jews, to the Samaritans, to the Gentiles, of all nations, kindreds and tongues. They gave in solemn charge to others to sound out and proclaim the glad tidings of great joy to all people. And need we ask, is not the Christian Church itself, in its own institution and constitution, virtually and essentially a missionary institution? Does not Paul formally state to the Thessalonians in his first epistle that from them sounded out the Word of the Lord not only in Macedonia and in Achaia, but in every place?

No man can really or truthfully enjoy the spiritual, the soul-stirring, the heart-reviving honors and felicities of the Christian institution and kingdom, who does not intelligently, cordially and efficiently espouse the missionary cause.

In other words, he must feel, he must have compassion for his fellow man; and, still further, he must practically sympathize with him in communicating to his spiritual necessities as well as to his physical wants and infirmities. The true ideal of all perfection—our blest and blissful Redeemer—went about continually doing good—to both the souls and the bodies of his fellow men; healing all that were, in body, soul or spirit, opprest by Satan, the enemy of God and of man.

To follow his example is the grand climax of humanity. It is not necessary to this end that he should occupy the pulpit. There are, as we conceive, myriads of Christian men in the private walks of life, who never aspired to the "sacred desk," that will far outshine, in eternal glory and blessedness, hosts of the reverend, the boasted and the boastful right reverend occupants of the sacred desks of this our day and generation.

But Solomon has furnished our motto:—"He that winneth" or taketh "souls is wise" (Prov. xi. 30). Was he not the wisest of men, the most potent and the richest of kings, that ever lived? He had, therefore, all the means and facilities of acquiring what we call knowledge—the knowledge of men and things; and, consequently, the value of men and things was legitimately within the area of his understanding; or, in this case, we might prefer to say, with all propriety, within the area of his comprehension.

Need I say that comprehension incomparably transcends apprehension? Simpletons may apprehend, but only wise men can comprehend anything. Solomon's rare gift was, that both his apprehension and his comprehension transcended those of all other men, and gave him a perspicacity and promptitude of decision never before or since possest by any man. His oracles, indeed, were the oracles of God. But God especially gave to him a power and opportunity of making one grand experiment and development for the benefit of his living contemporaries, and of all posterity, to whom God presents his biography, his Proverbs and his Ecclesiastes.

"The winning of souls" is, therefore, the richest and

best business, trade or calling, according to Solomon, ever undertaken or prosecuted by mortal man. Paul was fully aware of this, and therefore had always in his eye a "triple crown"—"a crown of righteousness," a "crown of life," a "crown of glory." And even in this life he had "a crown of rejoicing," in prospect of an exceeding and eternal weight of glory, imperishable in the heavens.

There is, too, a present reward, a present pleasure, a present joy and peace which the wisdom, and the riches, and the dignity, and the glory, and the honors of this world never did, never can, and consequently never will, confer on its most devoted and persevering votaries.

There is, indeed, a lawful and an honorable covetousness, which any and every Christian, man and woman, may cultivate and cherish.

Paul himself justifies the poetic license, when he says, "Covet earnestly the best gifts."

The best gifts in his horizon, however, were those which, when duly cultivated and employed, confer the greatest amount of profit and felicity upon others. We should, indeed, desire, even covet, the means and the opportunities of beatifying and aggrandizing one another with the true riches, the honors and the dignities that appertain to the spiritual, the heavenly and the eternal inheritance.

But we need not propound to your consideration or inquiry the claims—the paramount, the transcendent claims—which our enjoyment of the gospel and its soul-cheering, soul-animating, soul-enrapturing influences present to us as arguments and motives to extend and to animate its proclamation by every instrumentality and means which we can legitimately employ, to present it in all its attractions and claims upon the understanding, the conscience and the affections of our contemporaries, in our own country and in all others, as far as our most gracious and bountiful Benefactor affords the means and the opportunities of co-operating with Him, in the rescue and recovery of our fellow men, who, without such means and efforts, must forever perish, as aliens and enemies, in heart and in life, to God and to His divinely-commissioned ambassador, the glorious Messiah.

We plead for the original apostolic gospel and its positive institutions. If the great apostles Peter and Paul—the former to the Jews and the latter to the Gentiles—announced the true gospel of the grace of God, shall we hesitate a moment on the propriety and the necessity, divinely imposed upon us, of preaching the same gospel which they preached, and in advocating the same institutions which they established, under the plenary inspiration and direction of the Holy Spirit? Can we improve upon their institutions and enactments? What means that singular imperative enunciated by the evangelical prophet Isaiah (Isa. viii.), "Bind up the testimony, seal the law among my disciples?" What were its antecedents? Hearken! The prophet had just foretold. He, the subject of this oracle, viz: "The desire of all nations," was coming to be a sanctuary; but not a sanctuary alone, but for a stone of stumbling and a rock of offense (as at this day) to both the houses of Israel—for a gin and for a snare to the inhabitants of Jerusalem.

The Church, therefore, of right is, and ought to be, a great missionary society. Her parish is the whole earth, from sea to sea, and from the Euphrates to the last domicile of man.

But the crowning and consummating argument of the missionary cause has not been fully presented. There is but one word, in the languages of earth, that fully indicates it. And that word indicates neither less nor more than what is represented— literally, exactly, perspicuously represented—by the word philanthropy. But this being a Greek word needs, perhaps in some cases, an exact definition. And to make it memorable we will preface it with the statement of the fact that this word is found but twice in the Greek original New Testament (Acts xxviii., 2, and Titus iii., 4.). In the first passage this word is, in the common version, translated "kindness," and in the second, "love toward man." Literally and exactly, it signifies the love of man, objectively; but, more fully exprest, the love of one to another.

The love of God to man is one form of philanthropy; the love of angels to one man is another form of philanthropy; and the love of man to man, as such, is the true philanthropy of the law. It is not the love of one man to another man, because of favors received from him; this is only gratitude. It is not the love of one man to another man, because of a common country: this is mere patriotism. It is not the love of man to man, because of a common ancestry: this is mere natural affection. But it is the love of man to man, merely because he is a man. This is pure philanthropy. Such was the love of God to man as exhibited in the gift of His dearly beloved Son as a sin-offering for him. This is the name which the inspired writers of the New Testament give it. So Paul uses it, Titus iii. and iv. It should have been translated, "After that the kindness and philanthropy of God our Savior appeared." Again, Acts xxviii., 2, "The barbarous people of the Island of Melita showed us no little philanthropy.[3] They kindled a fire for us on their island, because of the impending rain and the cold."

There are, indeed, many forms and demonstrations of philanthropy. For one good man another good man might presume to die. But the philanthropy of God to man incomparably transcends all other forms of philanthropy known on earth or reported from heaven.

While we were sinners, in positive and actual rebellion against our Father and our God, He freely gave up His only begotten and dearly beloved Son, as a sin-offering for us, and laid upon Him, or placed in His account, the sin, the aggregate sin, of the world. He became in the hand of His Father and our Father a sin-offering for us. He took upon Himself, and His Father "laid upon him, the iniquity of us all." Was ever love like this? Angels of all ranks, spirits of all capacities, still contemplate it with

---

3 So we have always translated this term, in this passage.

increasing wonder and delight.

This gospel message is to be announced to all the world, to men of every nation under heaven. And this, too, with the promise of the forgiveness of sins and of a life everlasting in the heavens, to everyone who will cordially accept and obey it.

IRVING

PREPARATION FOR
CONSULTING THE ORACLES OF GOD

BIOGRAPHICAL NOTE

Edward Irving was born at Annan, Dumfriesshire, Scotland, in 1792. He was an early friend and lover of Jane Welsh, who afterwards married Thomas Carlyle. He showed ability at school, but had also a taste for the preaching of extreme Presbyterian seceders from the Church of Scotland. After graduating at the University of Edinburgh, in 1809, he began life by teaching school, but obtained a license to preach in 1815. He became assistant to Chalmers at Glasgow in 1819, where, great preacher as he was, he felt himself eclipsed by Chalmers, and in 1822 accepted the pulpit at a chapel in Hatton Garden, London. Here he leapt into fame. His melodious and resonant voice, his noble presence and the beauty of his features, enhanced the eloquence of his language. Eventually he became unbalanced by the adulation of the aristocratic and intellectual crowd that listened to him. They, however, grew tired of his prophecies and denunciations, and his eccentricities of judgment finally led to disruption, and "after a few years of futile but splendid evangelization, he died a broken-hearted man, tender and true to the last, altho the victim of unsubstantial religious vagaries." Carlyle wrote a touching memoir of his life. He died in 1834.

IRVING

1792-1834
PREPARATION FOR
CONSULTING THE ORACLES OF GOD

Search the scriptures.—John v., 39.

There was a time when each revelation of the word of God
had an introduction into this earth, which neither permitted
men to doubt whence it came, nor wherefore it was sent. If at the
giving of each several truth a star was not lighted up in heaven,
as at the birth of the Prince of Truth, there was done upon the
earth a wonder, to make her children listen to the message of
their Maker. The Almighty made bare His arm; and, through
mighty acts shown by His holy servants, gave demonstration of
His truth, and found for it a sure place among the other matters
of human knowledge and belief.

But now the miracles of God have ceased, and nature, secure
and unmolested, is no longer called on for testimonies to her
Creator's voice. No burning bush draws the footsteps to His
presence chamber; no invisible voice holds the ear awake; no
hand cometh forth from the obscurity to write His purposes in
letters of flame. The vision is shut up, and the testimony is sealed,
and the Word of the Lord is ended, and this solitary volume,
with its chapters and verses, is the sum total of all for which the
chariot of heaven made so many visits to the earth, and the Son
of God Himself tabernacled and dwelt among us.

The truth which it contains once dwelt undivulged in the
bosom of God; and, on coming forth to take its place among
things revealed, the heavens and the earth, and nature, through

85

all her chambers, gave reverent welcome. Beyond what it contains, the mysteries of the future are unknown. To gain it acceptation and currency, the noble company of martyrs testified unto the death. The general assembly of the first-born in heaven made it the day-star of their hopes, and the pavilion of their peace. Its every sentence is charmed with the power of God, and powerful to the everlasting salvation of souls.

Having our minds filled with these thoughts of the primeval divinity of revealed wisdom when she dwelt in the bosom of God, and was of His eternal Self a part, long before He prepared the heavens, or set a compass upon the face of the deep; revolving also how, by the space of four thousand years, every faculty of mute nature did solemn obeisance to this daughter of the Divine mind, whenever He pleased to commission her forth to the help of mortals; and further meditating upon the delights which she had of old with the sons of men, the height of heavenly temper to which she raised them, and the offspring of magnanimous deeds which these two—the wisdom of God, and the soul of man— did engender between themselves—meditating, I say, upon these mighty topics, our soul is smitten with grief and shame to remark how in this latter day she hath fallen from her high estate; and fallen along with her the great and noble character of men. Or, if there be still a few names, as of the missionary martyr, to emulate the saints of old—how to the commonalty of Christians her oracles have fallen into a household commonness, and her visits into a cheap familiarity; while by the multitude she is mistaken for a minister of terror sent to oppress poor mortals with moping melancholy, and inflict a wound upon the happiness of human kind.

For there is now no express stirring up the faculties to meditate her high and heavenly strains—there is no formal sequestration of the mind from all other concerns, on purpose for her special entertainment—there is no house of solemn seeking and solemn waiting for a spiritual frame, before entering and listening to the voice of the Almighty's wisdom. Who feels the sublime dignity there is in a saying, fresh descended from the porch of heaven? Who feels the awful weight there is in the least iota that hath dropped from the lips of God? Who feels the thrilling fear or trembling hope there is in words whereon the destinies of himself do hang? Who feels the swelling tide of gratitude within his breast, for redemption and salvation, instead of flat despair and everlasting retribution? Yea, that which is the guide and spur of all duty, the necessary aliment of Christian life, the first and the last of Christian knowledge and Christian feeling, hath, to speak the best, degenerated in these days to stand, rank and file, among those duties whereof it is parent, preserver, and commander. And, to speak not the best, but the fair and common truth, this book, the offspring of the Divine mind, and the perfection of heavenly wisdom, is permitted to lie from day to day, perhaps from week to week, unheeded and unperused, never welcome to our happy, healthy, and energetic moods; admitted, if admitted at all, in seasons of sickness, feeble-mindedness, and disabling sorrow. Yes, that which was sent to be a spirit of ceaseless joy and hope within the heart of man, is treated as the enemy of happiness, and the murderer of enjoyment; and eyed askance, as the remembrancer of death, and the very messenger of hell.

Oh! if books had but tongues to speak their wrongs, then might this book well exclaim: Hear, O heavens! and give ear, O earth! I came from the love and embrace of God, and mute nature, to whom I brought no boon, did me rightful homage. To men I come, and my words were to the children of men. I disclosed to you the mysteries hereafter, and the secrets of the throne of God. I set open to you the gates of salvation, and the way of eternal life, hitherto unknown. Nothing in heaven did I withhold from your hope and ambition; and upon your earthly lot I poured the full horn of Divine providence and consolation. But ye requited me with no welcome, ye held no festivity on my arrival; ye sequester me from happiness and heroism, closeting me with sickness and infirmity: ye make not of me, nor use me for, your guide to wisdom and prudence, but put me into a place in your last of duties, and withdraw me to a mere corner of your time; and most of ye set me at naught and utterly disregard me. I come, the fulness of the knowledge of God; angels delighted in my company, and desired to dive into my secrets. But ye, mortals, place masters over me, subjecting me to the discipline and dogmatism of men, and tutoring me in your schools of learning. I came, not to be silent in your dwellings, but to speak welfare to you and to your children. I came to rule, and my throne to set up in the hearts of men. Mine ancient residence was the bosom of God; no residence will I have but the soul of an immortal; and if you had entertained me, I should have possest you of the peace which I had with God, "when I was with Him and was daily His delight, rejoicing always before Him. Because I have called you and ye have refused, I have stretched out my hand and no man regarded; but ye have set at naught all my counsel and would none of my reproof; I also will laugh at your calamity, and mock when your fear cometh as desolation, and your destruction cometh as a whirlwind, when distress and anguish cometh upon you. Then shall they cry upon me, but I will not answer; they shall seek me early, but they shall not find me."

From this cheap estimation and wanton neglect of God's counsel, and from the terror of the curse consequent thereon, we have resolved, in the strength of God, to do our endeavor to deliver this congregation of His intelligent and worshiping people—an endeavor which we make with a full perception of the difficulties to be overcome on every side, within no less than without the sacred pale; and upon which we enter with the utmost diffidence of our powers, yet with the full purpose of straining them to the utmost, according to the measure with which it hath pleased God to endow our mind. And do Thou, O Lord, from whom cometh the perception of truth, vouchsafe to Thy servant an unction from Thine own Spirit, who searcheth all things, yes, the deep things of God; and vouchsafe to Thy people "the hearing ear and the understanding heart, that they may hear and understand, and their souls may live!"

Before the Almighty made His appearance upon Sinai, there were awful precursors sent to prepare His way; while He abode in sight, there were solemn ceremonies and a strict ritual of attendance; when He departed, the whole camp set itself to conform unto His revealed will. Likewise, before the Savior appeared, with His better law, there was a noble procession of seers and prophets, who decried and warned the world of His coming; when He came there were solemn announcements in the heavens and on the earth; He did not depart without due honors; and then followed, on His departure, a succession of changes and alterations which are still in progress, and shall continue in progress till the world's end. This may serve to teach us, that a revelation of the Almighty's will makes demand for these three things, on the part of those to whom it is revealed: A due preparation for receiving it; a diligent attention to it while it is disclosing; a strict observance of it when it is delivered.

In the whole book of the Lord's revelations you shall search in vain for one which is devoid of these necessary parts. Witness the awestruck Isaiah, while the Lord displayed before him the sublime pomp of His presence; and, not content with overpowering the frail sense of the prophet, dispatched a seraph to do the ceremonial of touching his lip with hallowed fire, all before He uttered one word into his astonished ear. Witness the majestic apparition to Saint John, in the Apocalypse, of all the emblematical glory of the Son of Man, allowed to take silent effect upon the apostle's spirit, and prepare it for the revelation of things to come. These heard with all their absorbed faculties, and with all their powers addrest them to the bidding of the Lord. But, if this was in aught flinched from, witness, in the persecution of the prophet Jonah, the fearful issues which ensued. From the presence of the Lord he could not flee. Fain would he have escaped to the uttermost parts of the earth; but in the mighty waters the terrors of the Lord fell upon him; and when engulfed in the deep, and entombed in the monster of the deep, still the Lord's word was upon the obdurate prophet, who had no rest, not the rest of the grave, till he had fulfilled it to the very uttermost.

Now, judging that every time we open the pages of this holy book, we are to be favored with no less than a communication from on high, in substance the same as those whereof we have detailed the three distinct and several parts, we conceive it due to the majesty of Him who speaks, that we, in like manner, discipline our spirits with a due preparation, and have them in proper frame, before we listen to the voice; that, while it is disclosing to us the important message, we be wrapt in full attention; and that, when it hath disburdened itself into our opened and enlarged spirits, we proceed forthwith to the business of its fulfilment, whithersoever and to whatsoever it summon us forth. Upon each of these three duties, incumbent upon one who would not forego the benefit of a heavenly message, we will discourse apart, addressing ourselves in this discourse to the first-mentioned of the three.

The preparation for the announcement.—"When God uttereth His voice," says the Psalmist, "coals of fire are kindled; the hills melt down like wax; the earth quakes; and deep proclaims itself unto hollow deep." These sensible images of the Creator have now vanished, and we are left alone, in the deep recesses of the meditative mind, to discern His coming forth. No trump of heaven now speaketh in the world's ear. No angelic conveyance of Heaven's will taketh shape from the vacant air; and having done his errand, retireth into his airy habitation. No human messenger putteth forth his miraculous hand to heal nature's unmedicable wounds, winning for his words a silent and astonished audience. Majesty and might no longer precede the oracles of Heaven. They lie silent and unobtrusive, wrapt up in their little compass, one volume among many, innocently handed to and fro, having no distinction but that in which our mustered thoughts are enabled to invest them. The want of solemn preparation and circumstantial pomp, the imagination of the mind hath now to supply. The presence of the Deity, and the authority of His voice, our thoughtful spirits must discern. Conscience must supply the terrors that were wont to go before Him; and the brightness of His coming, which the sense can no longer behold, the heart, ravished with His word, must feel.

For the solemn vocation of all her powers, to do her Maker honor and give Him welcome, it is, at the very least, necessary that the soul stand absolved from every call. Every foreign influence or authority arising out of the world, or the things of the world, should be burst when about to stand before the fountain of all authority; every argument, every invention, every opinion of man forgot, when about to approach to the Father and oracle of all intelligence. And as subjects, when their honors, with invitations, are held disengaged, tho preoccupied with a thousand appointments, so, upon an audience, fixt and about to be holden with the King of Kings, it will become the honored mortal to break loose from all thraldom of men and things, and be arrayed in liberty of thought and action to drink in the rivers of His pleasure, and to perform the mission of His lips.

Now far otherwise it hath appeared to us, that Christians as well as worldly men come to this most august occupation of listening to the word of God; preoccupied and prepossest, inclining to it a partial ear, and straitened understanding, and a disaffected will.

The Christian public are prone to preoccupy themselves with the admiration of those opinions by which they stand distinguished as a Church or sect from other Christians, and instead of being quite unfettered to receive the whole counsel of the Divinity, they are prepared to welcome it no further than it bears upon, and stands with opinions which they already favor. To this pre-judgment the early use of catechisms mainly contributes, which, however serviceable in their place, have the disadvantage of presenting the truth in a form altogether different from what it occupies in the world itself. In the one it is presented to the intellect chiefly (and in our catechisms to an intellect of a very subtle order), in the other it is presented more frequently to the heart, to the affections, to the emotions, to the fancy, and to all the faculties of the soul. In early youth, which is so applied to those compilations, an association takes place between religion and intellect, and a divorcement of religion from the other powers of the inner man. This derangement, judging from observation and experience, it is exceedingly difficult to put to rights in afterlife; and so it comes to pass, that in listening to the oracles of religion, the intellect is chiefly awake, and the better parts of the message—those which address the heart and its affections, those which dilate and enlarge our admiration of the Godhead, and those which speak to the various sympathies of our nature—we are, by the injudicious use of these narrow epitomes, disqualified to receive.

In the train of these comes controversy with its rough voice and unmeek aspect, to disqualify the soul for a full and fair audience of its Maker's word. The points of the faith we have been called on to defend, or which are reputable with our party, assume, in our esteem, an importance disproportionate to their importance in the Word, which we come to relish chiefly when it goes to sustain them, and the Bible is hunted for arguments and texts of controversy, which are treasured up for future service. The solemn stillness which the soul should hold before his Maker, so favorable to meditation and rapt communion with the throne of God, is destroyed at every turn by suggestions of what is orthodox and evangelical—where all is orthodox and evangelical; the spirit of such readers becomes lean, being fed with abstract truths and formal propositions; their temper uncongenial, being ever disturbed with controversial suggestions; their prayers undevout recitals of their opinions; their discourse technical announcements of their faith. Intellect, old intellect, hath the sway over heavenward devotion and holy fervor. Man, contentious man, hath the attention which the unsearchable God should undivided have; and the fine, full harmony of heaven's melodious voice, which, heard apart, were sufficient to lap the soul in ecstasies unspeakable, is jarred and interfered with, and the heavenly spell is broken by the recurring conceits, sophisms, and passions of men. Now truly an utter degradation it is of the Godhead to have His word in league with that of man, or any council of men. What matter to me whether the Pope, or any work of any mind, be exalted to the quality of God? If any helps are to be imposed for the understanding, or safeguarding, or sustaining of the word, why not the help of statues and pictures of my devotions? Therefore, while the warm fancies of the Southerns have given their idolatry to the ideal forms of noble art, let us Northerns beware we give not our idolatry to the cold and coarse abstractions of human intellect.

For the preoccupations of worldly minds, they are not to be reckoned up, being manifold as their favorite passions and pursuits. One thing only can be said, that before coming to the oracles of God they are not preoccupied with the expectation and fear of Him. No chord in their heart is in unison with things unseen; no moments are set apart for religious thought and meditation; no anticipations of the honored interview; no prayer of preparation like that of Daniel before Gabriel was sent to teach him; no devoutness like that of Cornelius before the celestial visitation; no fastings like that of Peter before the revelation of the glory of the Gentiles! Now to minds which are not attuned to holiness, the words of God find no entrance, striking heavy on the ear, seldom making way to the understanding, almost never to the heart. To spirits hot with conversation, perhaps heady with argument, uncomposed by solemn thought, but ruffled and in uproar from the concourse of worldly interests, the sacred page may be spread out, but its accents are drowned in the noise which hath not yet subsided in the breast. All the awe, and pathos, and awakened consciousness of a Divine approach, imprest upon the ancients by the procession of solemnities, is to worldly men without a substitute. They have not yet solicited themselves to be in readiness. In a usual mood and vulgar frame they come to God's word as to other compositions, reading it without any active imaginations about Him who speaks; feeling no awe of a sovereign Lord, nor care of a tender Father, nor devotion to a merciful Savior. Nowise deprest themselves out of their wonted dependence, nor humiliated before the King of Kings—no prostrations of the soul, nor falling at His feet as dead—no exclamation, as of Isaiah, "Wo is me, for I am of unclean lips!"—no request "Send me"—nor fervent ejaculation of welcome, as of Samuel, "Lord, speak, for Thy servant heareth!" Truly they feel toward His word much as to the word of an equal. No wonder it shall fail of happy influence upon the spirits which have, as it were, on purpose, disqualified themselves for its benefits by removing from the regions of thought and feeling which it accords with, into other regions, which it is of too severe dignity to affect, otherwise than with stern menace and direful foreboding! If they would have it bless them and do them good, they must change their manner of approaching it, and endeavor to bring themselves into that prepared, and collected, and reverential frame which becomes an interview with the High and Holy One who inhabiteth the praises of eternity.

Having thus spoken without equivocation, and we hope without offense, to the contradictoriness and preoccupation with which Christians and worldly men are apt to come to the perusal of the Word of God, we shall now set forth the two master-feelings under which we shall address ourselves to the sacred occupation.

It is a good custom, inherited from the hallowed days of Scottish piety, and in our cottages still preserved, tho in our cities generally given up, to preface the morning and evening worship of the family with a short invocation of blessing from the Lord. This is in unison with the practise and recommendation of pious men, never to open the Divine Word without a silent invocation of the Divine Spirit. But no address to heaven is of any virtue, save as it is the expression of certain pious sentiments with which the mind is full and overflowing. Of those sentiments which befit the mind that comes into conference with its Maker, the first and most prominent should be gratitude for His ever having condescended to hold commerce with such wretched and fallen creatures. Gratitude not only expressing itself in proper terms, but possessing the mind with one abiding and over-mastering mood, under which it shall sit imprest the whole duration of the interview. Such an emotion as can not utter itself in language—tho by language it indicates its presence—but keeps us in a devout and adoring frame, while the Lord is uttering His voice.

Go visit a desolate widow with consolation, and help, and fatherhood of her orphan children—do it again and again—and your presence, the sound of your approaching footstep, the soft utterance of your voice, the very mention of your name, shall come to dilate her heart with a fulness which defies her tongue to utter, but speaking by the tokens of a swimming eye, and clasped hands, and fervent ejaculations to heaven upon your head! No less copious acknowledgment of God, the author of our well-being, and the Father of our better hopes, ought we to feel when His Word discloseth to us the excess of His love. Tho a veil be now cast over the Majesty which speaks, it is the voice of the Eternal which we hear, coming in soft cadences to win our favor, yet omnipotent as the voice of the thunder, and overpowering as the rushing of many waters. And tho the evil of the future intervene between our hand and the promised goods, still are they from His lips who speaks, and it is done, who commands, and all things stand fast. With no less emotion, therefore, should this book be opened, than if, like him in the Apocalypse, you saw the voice which spake; or, like him in the trance, you were into the third heaven translated, companying and communing with the realities of glory which the eye hath not seen, nor ear heard, nor the heart of man conceived.

Far and foreign from such an opened and awakened bosom is that cold and formal hand which is generally laid upon the sacred volume; that unfeeling and unimpressive tone with which its accents are pronounced; and that listless and incurious ear into which its blessed sounds are received. How can you, thus unimpassioned, hold communion with themes in which everything awful, vital, and endearing meet together? Why is not curiosity, curiosity ever hungry, on edge to know the doings and intentions of Jehovah, King of Kings? Why is not interest, interest ever awake, on tip-toe to hear the future destiny of itself? Why is not the heart, that panteth over the world after love and friendship, overpowered with the full tide of the divine acts and expressions of love? Where is nature gone when she is not moved with the tender mercy of Christ? Methinks the affections of men are fallen into the yellow leaf. Of the poets which charm the world's ear, who is he that inditeth a song unto his God? Some will tune their harps to sensual pleasure, and by the enchantment of their genius well-nigh commend their unholy themes to the imagination of saints. Others, to the high and noble sentiments of the heart, will sing of domestic joys and happy unions, casting around sorrow the radiancy of virtue, and bodying forth, in undying forms, the short-lived visions of joy! Others have enrolled themselves the high-priests of mute nature's charms, enchanting her echoes with their minstrelsy, and peopling her solitudes with the bright creatures of their fancy. But when, since the days of the blind master of English song, hath any poured forth a lay worthy of the Christian theme? Nor in philosophy, "the palace of the soul," have men been more mindful of their Maker. The flowers of the garden and the herbs of the field have their unwearied devotees, crossing the ocean, wayfaring in the desert, and making devout pilgrimages to every region of nature for offerings to their patron muse. The rocks, from their residences among the clouds to their deep rests in the dark bowels of the earth, have a bold and most venturous priesthood, who see in their rough and flinty faces a more delectable image to adore than in the revealed countenance of God. And the political warfare of the world is a very Moloch, who can at any time command his hecatomb of human victims. But the revealed suspense of God, to which the harp of David, and the prophetic lyre of Isaiah were strung, the prudence of God, which the wisest of men coveted after, preferring it to every gift which heaven could confer, and the eternal intelligence Himself in human form, and the unction of the Holy One which abideth—these the common heart of man hath forsaken, and refused to be charmed withal.

I testify, that there ascendeth not from earth a hosanna of her children to bear witness in the ear of the upper regions to the wonderful manifestations of her God! From a few scattered hamlets in a small portion of her territory a small voice ascendeth, like the voice of one crying in the wilderness. But to the service of our general Preserver there is no concourse, from Dan unto Beersheba, of our people, the greater part of whom, after two thousand years of apostolic commission, have not the testimonials of our God; and the multitude of those who disrespect or despise them!

But, to return from this lamentation, which may God hear, who doth not disregard the cries of His afflicted people! With the full sense of obligation to the giver, combine a humble sense of your own incapacity to value and to use the gift of His oracles. Having no taste whatever for the mean estimates which are made, and the coarse invectives that are vented, against human nature, which, tho true in the main, are often in the manner so unfeeling and triumphant, as to reveal hot zeal rather than tender and deep sorrow, we will not give in to this popular strain. And yet it is a truth by experience, revealed, that tho there be in man most noble faculties, and a nature restless after the knowledge and truth of things, there are toward God and His revealed will an indisposition and a regardlessness, which the most tender and enlightened consciences are the most ready to acknowledge. Of our emancipated youth, who, bound after the knowledge of the visible works of God, and the gratification of the various instincts of nature, how few betake themselves at all, how few absorb themselves with the study and obedience of the Word of God! And when, by God's visitation, we address ourselves to the task, how slow is our progress and how imperfect our performance! It is most true that nature is unwilling to the subject of the Scriptures. The soul is previously possest with adverse interests; the world hath laid an embargo on her faculties, and monopolized them to herself; old habit hath perhaps added to his almost incurable callousness; and the enemy of God and man is skilful to defend what he hath already won. So circumstanced, and every man is so circumstanced, we come to the audience of the Word of God, and listen in the worse tune than a wanton to a sermon, or a hardened knave to a judicial address. Our understanding is prepossest with a thousand idols of the world—religious or irreligious—which corrupt the reading of the Word into a straining of the text to their service, and when it will not strain, cause it to be skimmed, and perhaps despised or hated. Such a thing as a free and unlimited reception of all parts of the Scripture into the mind, is a thing most rare to be met with, and when met with will be found the result of many a sore submission of nature's opinions as well as of nature's likings.

But the Word, as hath been said, is not for the intellect alone, but for the heart, and for the will. Now if any one be so wedded to his own candor as to think he doth accept the divine truth unabated, surely no one will flatter himself into the belief that his heart is attuned and enlarged for all divine commandments. The man who thus misdeems of himself must, if his opinions were just, be like a sheet of fair paper, unblotted and unwritten on; whereas all men are already occupied, to the very fulness, with other opinions and attachments and desires than the Word reveals. We do not grow Christians by the same culture by which we grow men, otherwise what need of divine revelation, and divine assistance? But being unacquainted from the womb with God, and attached to what is seen and felt, through early and close acquaintance, we are ignorant and detached from what is unseen and unfelt. The Word is a novelty to our nature, its truths fresh truths, its affections fresh affections, its obedience gathered from the apprehension of nature and the commerce of the worldly life. Therefore there needeth, in one that would be served from this storehouse opened by heaven, a disrelish of his old acquisitions, and a preference of the new, a simple, child-like teachableness, an allowance of ignorance and error, with whatever else beseems an anxious learner. Coming to the Word of God, we are like children brought into the conversations of experienced men; and we should humbly listen and reverently inquire; or we are like raw rustics introduced into high and polished life, and we should unlearn our coarseness, and copy the habits of the station; nay we are like offenders caught, and for the moment committed to the bosom of honorable society, with the power of regaining our lost condition and inheriting honor and trust—therefore we should walk softly and tenderly, covering our former reproach with modesty and humbleness, hasting to redeem our reputation by distinguished performances, against offense doubly guarded, doubly watchful for dangerous and extreme positions to demonstrate our recovered goodness.

These two sentiments—devout veneration of God for His unspeakable gift, and deep distrust of our capacity to estimate and use it aright—will generate in the mind a constant aspiration after the guidance and instruction of a higher power; the first sentiment of goodness remembered, emboldening us to draw near to Him who first drew near to us, and who with Christ will not refuse us any gift; the second sentiment, of weakness remembered, teaching us our need, and prompting us by every interest of religion and every feeling of helplessness to seek of Him who hath said, "If any one lack wisdom let him ask God, who giveth liberally and upbraideth not." The soul which under these two master-feelings cometh to read, shall not read without profit. Every new revelation, feeding his gratitude and nourishing his former ignorance, will confirm the emotions he is under, and carry them onward to an unlimited dimension. Such a one will prosper in the way; enlargement of the inner man will be his portion and the establishment in the truth his exceeding great reward. "In the strength of the Lord shall his right hand get victory—even in the name of the Lord of Hosts. His soul shall also flourish with the fruits of righteousness from the seed of the word, which liveth and abideth forever."

Thus delivered from prepossessions of all other masters, and arrayed in the raiment of humility and love, the soul should advance to the meeting of her God; and she should call a muster of her faculties and have all her poor grace in attendance, and anything she knows of His excellent works and exalted ways she should summon up to her remembrance; her understanding she should quicken, her memory refresh, her imagination stimulate, her affections cherish, and her conscience arouse. All that is within her should be stirred up, her whole glory should awake and her whole beauty display itself for the meeting of her King. As His hand-maiden she should meet Him; His own handiwork, tho sore defaced, yet seeking restoration; His humble, because offending, servant—yet nothing slavish, tho humble—nothing superstitious, tho devout—nothing tame, tho modest in her demeanor; but quick and ready, all addrest and wound up for her Maker's will.

How different the ordinary proceeding of Christians, who, with timorous, mistrustful spirits, with an abeyance of intellect, and a dwarfish reduction of their natural powers, enter to the conference of the Word of God! The natural powers of man are to be mistrusted, doubtless, as the willing instruments of the evil one; but they must be honored also as the necessary instruments of the Spirit of God, whose operation is a dream, if it be not through knowledge, intellect, conscience, and action. Now Christians, heedless of the grand resurrection of the mighty instruments of thought and action, at the same time coveting hard after holy attainment, do often resign the mastery of themselves, and are taken into the counsel of the religious world—whirling around the eddy of some popular leader—and so drifted, I will not say from godliness, but drifted certainly from that noble, manly and independent course, which, under steerage of the Word of God, they might safely have pursued for the precious interests of their immortal souls. Meanwhile these popular leaders, finding no necessity for strenuous endeavors and high science in the ways of God, but having a gathering host to follow them, deviate from the ways of deep and penetrating thought—refuse the contest with the literary and accomplished enemies of the faith—bring a contempt upon the cause in which mighty men did formerly gird themselves to the combat—and so cast the stumbling-block of a mistaken paltryness between enlightened men and the cross of Christ! So far from this simple-mindedness (but its proper name is feeble-mindedness), Christians should be—as aforetime in this island they were wont to be—the princes of human intellect, the lights of the world, the salt of the political and social state. Till they come forth from the swaddling-bands, in which foreign schools have girt them, and walk boldly upon the high places of human understanding, they shall never obtain that influence in the upper regions of knowledge and power, of which, unfortunately, they have not the apostolic unction to be in quest. They will never be the master and commanding spirit of the time, until they cast off the wrinkled and withered skin of an obsolete old age, and clothe themselves with intelligence as with a garment, and bring forth the fruits of power and love and of a sound mind.

Mistake us not, for we steer in a narrow, very narrow channel, with rocks of popular prejudice on every side. While we thus invoke to the reading of the Word, the highest strains of the human soul, mistake us not as derogating from the office of the Spirit of God. Far be it from any Christian, much further from any Christian pastor, to withdraw from God the honor which is everywhere His due; but there most of all His due where the human mind labored alone for thousands of years, and labored with no success—viz., the regeneration of itself, and its restoration to the last semblance of the divinity! Oh! let him be reverently inquired after, devoutly meditated on, and most thankfully acknowledged in every step of progress from the soul's fresh awakening out of her dark, oblivious sleep—even to her ultimate attainment upon earth and full accomplishment for heaven. And there may be a fuller choir of awakened men to advance His honor and glory here on earth, and hereafter in heaven above; let the saints bestir themselves like angels and the ministers of religion like archangels strong! And now at length let us have a demonstration made of all that is noble in thought, and generous in action, and devoted in piety, for bestirring this lethargy, and breaking the bonds of hell, and redeeming the whole world to the service of its God and King!

ARNOLD

ALIVE IN GOD

BIOGRAPHICAL NOTE

Thomas Arnold, schoolmaster and preacher, was born at West Cowes, Isle of Wight, in 1795. He was educated at Oxford, and after his graduation taught as fellow of Oriel College, until in 1820 he removed to Laleham near Haines and took pupils to prepare for the universities. In 1827 he was elected to the head mastership of Rugby, and took priest's orders before entering upon his duties. At Rugby he remained till his death in 1842. His great work as an educator consisted in teaching boys the duty of self-government, self-control and freedom of intellectual judgement. His sermons in the school chapel were distinguished by simplicity and profound moral and religious earnestness.

ARNOLD

1795-1842
ALIVE IN GOD

God is not the God of the dead, but of the living.—Matt. xxii., 32.

We hear these words as a part of our Lord's answer to the Sadducees; and as their question was put in evident profaneness, and the answer to it is one which to our minds is quite obvious and natural, so we are apt to think that in this particular story there is less than usual that particularly concerns us. But it so happens that our Lord in answering the Sadducees has brought in one of the most universal and most solemn of all truths,— which is indeed implied in many parts of the Old Testament, but which the Gospel has revealed to us in all its fulness,—the truth contained in the words of the text, that "God is not the God of the dead, but of the living."

I would wish to unfold a little what is contained in these words which we often hear, even, perhaps, without quite understanding them, and many times oftener without fully entering into them. And we may take them, without fully entering into them. And we may take them, first, in their first part, where they say that "God is not the God of the dead."

The word "dead," we know, is constantly used in Scripture in a double sense, as meaning those who are dead spiritually as well as those who are dead naturally. And in either sense the words are alike applicable: "God is not the God of the dead."

God's not being the God of the dead signifies two things: that they who are without Him are dead, as well as that they who are dead are also without Him. So far as our knowledge goes respecting inferior animals they appear to be examples of this truth. They appear to us to have no knowledge of God; and we are not told that they have any other life than the short one of which our senses inform us. I am well aware that our ignorance of their condition is so great that we may not dare to say anything of them positively; there may be a hundred things true respecting them which we neither know nor imagine. I would only say that according to that most imperfect light in which we see them the two points of which I have been speaking appear to meet in them: we believe that they have no consciousness of God, and we believe that they will die. And so far, therefore, they afford an example of the agreement, if I may so speak, between these two points; and were intended, perhaps, to be to our view a continual image of it. But we had far better speak of ourselves. And here, too, it is the case that "God is not the God of the dead." If we are without Him we are dead, and if we are dead we are without Him; in other words, the two ideas of death and absence from God are in fact synonymous.

Thus, in the account given of the fall of man, the sentence of death and of being cast out of Eden go together; and if any one compares the description of the second Eden in the Revelation, and recollects how especially it is there said that God dwells in the midst of it, and is its light by day and night, he will see that the banishment from the first Eden means a banishment from the presence of God. And thus, in the day that Adam sinned he died; for he was cast out of Eden immediately, however long he may have moved about afterward upon the earth where God was not. And how very strong to the same point are the words of Hezekiah's prayer, "The grave cannot praise Thee, Death cannot celebrate Thee; they that go down into the pit cannot hope for Thy truth"; words which express completely the feeling that God is not the God of the dead. This, too, appears to be the sense generally of the expression used in various parts of the Old Testament, "Thou shalt surely die."

It is, no doubt, left purposely obscure; nor are we ever told in so many words all that is meant by death; but, surely, it always implies a separation from God, and the being—whatever the notion may extend to—the being dead to Him.

Thus, when David had committed his great sin and had expressed his repentance for it, Nathan tells him, "The Lord also hath put away thy sin; thou shalt not die"; which means most expressively, thou shalt not die to God.

In one sense David died, as all men die; nor was he by any means freed from the punishment of his sin; he was not, in that sense, forgiven, but he was allowed still to regard God as his God; and therefore his punishments were but fatherly chastisements from God's hand, designed for his profit that he might be partaker of God's holiness.

And thus altho Saul was sentenced to lose his kingdom, and altho he was killed with his sons on Mount Gilboa, yet I do not think that we find the sentence passed upon him, "Thou shalt surely die"; and therefore we have no right to say that God had ceased to be his God altho He visited him with severe chastisements and would not allow him to hand down to his sons the crown of Israel. Observe also the language of the eighteenth chapter of Ezekiel, where the expressions occur so often, "He shall surely live," and "He shall surely die."

We have no right to refer these to a mere extension on the one hand, or a cutting short on the other, of the term of earthly existence. The promise of living long in the land or, as in Hezekiah's case, of adding to his days fifteen years, is very different from the full and unreserved blessing, "Thou shalt surely live." And we know, undoubtedly, that both the good and the bad to whom Ezekiel spoke died alike the natural death of the body. But the peculiar force of the promise and of the threat was, in the one case, Thou shalt belong to God; in the other, Thou shalt cease to belong to Him; although the veil was not yet drawn up which concealed the full import of those terms, "belonging to God," and "ceasing to belong to Him": nay, can we venture to affirm that it is fully drawn aside even now?

I have dwelt on this at some length, because it really seems to place the common state of the minds of too many amongst us in a light which is exceedingly awful; for if it be true, as I think the Scripture implies, that to be dead and to be without God are precisely the same thing, then can it be denied that the symptoms of death are strongly marked upon many of us? Are there not many who never think of God or care about His service? Are there not many who live, to all appearance, as unconscious of His existence, as we fancy the inferior animals to be?

And is it not quite clear that to such persons God cannot be said to be their God? He may be the God of heaven and earth, the God of the universe, the God of Christ's Church; but He is not their God, for they feel to have nothing at all to do with Him; and therefore, as He is not their God, they are, and must be according to the Scripture, reckoned among the dead.

But God is the God "of the living." That is, as before, all who are alive live unto Him; all who live unto Him are alive. "God said, I am the God of Abraham, and the God of Isaac, and the God of Jacob"; and therefore, says our Lord, "Abraham, and Isaac, and Jacob are not and cannot be dead." They cannot be dead, because God owns them: He is not ashamed to be called their God; therefore they are not cast out from Him; therefore, by necessity, they live.

Wonderful, indeed, is the truth here implied, in exact agreement, as we have seen, with the general language of Scripture; that, as she who but touched the hem of Christ's garment was in a moment relieved from her infirmity, so great was the virtue which went out from Him; so they who are not cast out from God, but have anything whatever to do with Him, feel the virtue of His gracious presence penetrating their whole nature; because He lives, they must live also.

Behold, then, life and death set before us; not remote (if a few years be, indeed, to be called remote), but even now present before us; even now suffered or enjoyed. Even now, we are alive unto God, or dead unto God; and, as we are either the one or the other, so we are, in the highest possible sense of the terms, alive or dead. In the highest possible sense of the terms; but who can tell what that highest possible sense of the terms is? So much has, indeed, been revealed to us, that we know now that death means a conscious and perpetual death, as life means a conscious and perpetual life.

But greatly, indeed, do we deceive ourselves, if we fancy that, by having thus much told us, we have also risen to the infinite heights, or descended to the infinite depths, contained in those little words, life and death. They are far higher, and far deeper, than ever thought or fancy of man has reached to. But, even on the first edge of either, at the visible beginnings of that infinite ascent or descent, there is surely something which may give us a foretaste of what is beyond. Even to us in this mortal state, even to you, advanced but so short a way on your very earthly journey, life and death have a meaning: to be dead unto God, or to be alive to Him, are things perceptibly different.

For, let me ask of those who think least of God, who are most separate from Him, and most without Him, whether there is not now actually, perceptibly, in their state, something of the coldness, the loneliness, the fearfulness of death? I do not ask them whether they are made unhappy by the fear of God's anger; of course they are not: for they who fear God are not dead to Him, nor He to them.

The thought of Him gives them no disquiet at all; this is the very point we start from. But I would ask them whether they know what it is to feel God's blessing. For instance: we all of us have our troubles of some sort or other, our disappointments, if not our sorrows. In these troubles, in these disappointments,—I care not how small they may be,—have they known what it is to feel that God's hand is over them; that these little annoyances are but His fatherly correction; that He is all the time loving us, and supporting us? In seasons of joy, such as they taste very often, have they known what it is to feel that they are tasting the kindness of their heavenly Father, that their good things come from His hand and are but an infinitely slight foretaste of His love? Sickness, danger; I know that they come to many of us but rarely; but if we have known them, or at least sickness, even in its lighter form, if not in its graver,—have we felt what it is to know that we are in our Father's hands, that He is with us, and will be with us to the end; that nothing can hurt those whom He loves?

Surely, then, if we have never tasted anything of this: if in trouble, or in joy, or in sickness, we are left wholly to ourselves to bear as we can and enjoy as we can; if there is no voice that ever speaks out of the heights and the depths around us to give any answer to our own; if we are thus left to ourselves in this vast world,—there is in this a coldness and a loneliness; and whenever we come to be, of necessity, driven to be with our own hearts alone, the coldness and the loneliness must be felt. But consider that the things which we see around us cannot remain with us nor we with them. The coldness and loneliness of the world, without God, must be felt more and more as life wears on; in every change of our own state, in every separation from or loss of a friend, in every more sensible weakness of our own bodies, in every additional experience of the uncertainty of our own counsels,—the deathlike feeling will come upon us more and more strongly: we shall gain more of that fearful knowledge which tells us that "God is not the God of the dead."

And so, also, the blessed knowledge that He is the God "of the living" grows upon those who are truly alive. Surely He "is not far from every one of us." No occasion of life fails to remind those who live unto Him that He is their God and that they are His children. On light occasions or on grave ones, in sorrow and in joy, still the warmth of His love is spread, as it were, all through the atmosphere of their lives; they forever feel His blessing. And if it fills them with joy unspeakable even now, when they so often feel how little they deserve it; if they delight still in being with God, and in living to Him, let them be sure that they have in themselves the unerring witness of life eternal: God is the God of the living, and all who are with Him must live.

Hard it is, I well know, to bring this home in any degree to the minds of those who are dead; for it is of the very nature of the dead that they can hear no words of life. But it has happened that, even whilst writing what I have just been uttering to you, the news reached me that one who two months ago was one of your number, who this very half-year has shared in all the business and amusements of this place, is passed already into that state where the meanings of the terms life and death are become fully revealed. He knows what it is to live unto God and what it is to die to Him. Those things which are to us unfathomable mysteries are to him all plain: and yet but two months ago he might have thought himself as far from attaining this knowledge as any of us can do. Wherefore it is clear that these things, life and death, may hurry their lesson upon us sooner than we deem of, sooner than we are prepared to receive it. And that were indeed awful, if, being dead to God, and yet little feeling it because of the enjoyments of our worldly life, those enjoyments were on a sudden to be struck away from us, and we should find then that to be dead to God was death indeed, a death from which there is no waking, and in which there is no sleeping forever.

WAYLAND

A DAY IN THE LIFE OF JESUS OF NAZARETH

BIOGRAPHICAL NOTE

Francis Wayland, preacher and philosopher, was born in New York, in 1796. He graduated at Union College in 1813 and in 1816 entered Hudson Theological Seminary. His first charge was the First Baptist Church in Boston. Here he established his reputation as an able and vigorous pulpit orator. Five years later he accepted a chair in Union College, but in 1827 entered upon an incumbency of twenty-eight years as President of Brown University, Providence. This institution he built up on a broad and liberal basis, quite emancipating it from narrow sectarianism. In 1855 he became pastor of the First Baptist Church in Providence and died in 1865.

WAYLAND

1796-1865

A DAY IN THE LIFE OF JESUS OF NAZARETH

And the apostles, when they were returned, told him all that they had done. And he took them, and went aside privately into a desert place, belonging to the city called Bethsaida. And the people when they knew it, followed him: and he received them, and spake unto them of the kingdom of God, and healed them that had need of healing. And when the day began to wear away, then came the twelve, and said unto him, Send the multitude away, that they may go into the towns and country round about, and lodge and get victuals: for we are here in a desert place. But he said unto them, Give ye them to eat. And they said, We have no more but five loaves and two fishes; except we should go and buy meat for all this people. For they were about five thousand men. And he said to his disciples, Make them sit down by fifties in a company. And they did so, and made them all sit down. Then he took the five loaves and the two fishes and looking up to heaven, he blessed them and brake, and gave to the disciples to set before the multitude. And they did eat, and were all filled: and there was taken up of fragments that remained to them twelve baskets.
—Luke ix., 10-17.

It was the sagacious opinion of, I think, the late Professor Porson, that he would rather see a single copy of a daily newspaper of ancient Athens, than read all the commentaries upon the Grecian tragedies that have ever been written. The reason for this preference is obvious. A single sheet, similar to our daily newspapers, published in the time of Pericles, would admit us at

115

once to a knowledge of the habits, manners, modes of opinion, political relations, social condition, and moral attainments of the people, such as we never could gain from the study of all the writers that have ever attempted to illustrate the nature of Grecian civilization.

The same remark is true in respect to our knowledge of the character of individuals who have lived in a former age. What would we not, at the present day, give for a few pages of the private diary of Julius Cesar, or Cicero, or Brutus, or Augustus; or for the minute reminiscences of any one who had spent a few days in the company of either of these distinguished men? What a flood of life would the discovery of such a manuscript throw upon Roman life, but especially upon the private opinions, the motives, the aspirations, the moral estimates of the men whose names have become household words throughout the world! A few such pages might, perchance, dissipate the authority of many a bulky folio on which we now rely with implicit confidence. Not only would the characters of these heroes of antiquity stand out in bolder relief than they have ever done before, but the individuals themselves would be brought within the range of our personal sympathy; and we should seem to commune with them as we do with an intimate acquaintance.

It is worthy of remark, that we are favored with a larger portion of this kind of information, respecting Jesus of Nazareth, than almost any other distinguished person that has ever lived. He left no writings Himself; hence all that we know of Him has been written by others. The narrators, however, were the personal attendants, and not the mere auditors or pupils of their master. The apostles were members of the family of Jesus; they traveled with Him, on foot, throughout the length and breadth of Palestine; they partook with Him of his frugal meals, and bore with Him the trial of hunger, weariness, and want of shelter; they followed Him through the lonely wilderness and the crowded street; they saw His miracles in every variety of form, and listened to His discourses in public as well as to His explanations in private. Hence their whole narrative is instinct with life; a vivid picture of Jewish manners and customs, rendered more definite and characteristic by the moral light which then, for the first time, shone upon it. Hence it is that these few pages are replete with moral lessons that never weary us in the perusal, and which have been the source of unfailing illumination to all succeeding ages.

The verses which I have read, as the text of this discourse, may well be taken as an illustration of all that I have here said. They may, without impropriety, be styled a day in the life of Jesus of Nazareth. By observing the manner in which our blessed Lord spent a single day, we may form some conception of the kind of life which He ordinarily led; and we may, perchance, treasure up some lessons which it were well if we should exemplify in our daily practice.

The place at which these events occurred was near the head of the Sea of Galilee, where it receives the waters of the upper Jordan. This was one of the Savior's favorite places of resort. Capernaum, Chorazin, and Bethsaida, all in this immediate vicinity, are always spoken of in the gospels as towns which enjoyed the largest share of His ministerial labors, and were distinguished most frequently with the honor of His personal presence. The scenery of the neighborhood is wild and romantic. To the north and west, the eye rests on the lofty summits of Lebanon and Hermon. To the south, there opens upon the view the blue expanse of the lake, enclosed by frowning rocks, which here and there jut over far into the waters, and then again retire towards the land, leaving a level beach to invite the labors of the fishermen. The people, removed at a considerable distance from the metropolis of Judea, cultivated those rural habits with which the simple tastes of the Savior would most readily harmonize. Near this spot was also one of the most frequented fords of the Jordan, on the road from Damascus to Jerusalem; and thus, while residing here, He enjoyed unusual facilities for disseminating throughout this whole region a knowledge of those truths which

117

He came on earth to promulgate.

Some weeks previous to the time in which the events spoken of in the text occurred, our Lord had sent His disciples to announce the approach of the kingdom of heaven, in all the cities and villages which He Himself proposed to visit. He conferred on them the power to work miracles, in attestation of their authority, and of the divine character of Him by whom they were sent. He imposed upon them strict rules of conduct, and directed them to make known to every one who would hear them the good news of the coming dispensation. As soon as He sent them forth, He Himself went immediately abroad to teach and to preach in their cities. As their Master and Lord, He might reasonably have claimed exemption from the personal toil and the rigid self-denials to which they were by necessity subjected. But He had laid no claim to such exemption. He commenced without delay the performance of the very same duties which He had imposed upon them. He felt himself under obligation to set an example of obedience to His own rules. "The Son of Man," said He, "came not to be ministered unto, but to minister, and to give His life a ransom for many." "Which," said He, "is greater, he that sitteth at meat, or he that serveth? but I am among you as He that serveth." Would it not be well, if, in this respect, we copied more minutely the example of our Lord, and held ourselves responsible for the performance of the very same duties which we so willingly impose upon our brethren? We best prove that we believe an act obligatory, when we commence the performance of it ourselves. Many zealous Christians employ themselves in no other labor than that of urging their brethren to effort. Our Savior acted otherwise. In this respect, His example is specially to be imitated by His ministers. When they urge upon others a moral duty, they must be the first to perform it. When they inculcate an act of self-denial, they themselves must make the noblest sacrifice. Can we conceive of anything which could so much increase the moral power of the ministry, and rouse to a flame the dormant energy of the churches, as obedience to this teaching of Christ by the preachers of His gospel?

It seems that the Savior had selected a well-known spot, at the head of the lake, for the place of meeting for his apostles, after this their first missionary tour had been completed. "The apostles gathered themselves unto Jesus, and told Him all things, both what they had done, and what they had taught." There is something delightful in this filial confidence which these simple-hearted men reposed in their almighty Redeemer. They told Him of their success and their failure, of their wisdom and their folly, of their reliance and their unbelief. We can almost imagine ourselves spectators of this meeting between Christ and them, after this their first separation from each other. The place appointed was most probably some well-known locality on the shore of the lake, under the shadow of its overhanging rocks, where the cool air from the bosom of the water refreshed each returning laborer, as he came back beaten out with the fatigues of travel, under the burning sun of Syria. You can imagine the joy with which each drew near to the Master, after this temporary absence; and the honest greetings with which every newcomer was welcomed by those who had chanced to arrive before him. We can seem to perceive the Savior of men listening with affectionate earnestness to the recital of their various adventures; and interposing, from time to time, a word either of encouragement or of caution, as the character and circumstances of each narrator required it. The bosom of each was unveiled before the Searcher of Hearts, and the consolation which each one needed was bestowed upon him abundantly. The toilsomeness of their journey was no longer remembered, as each one received from the Son of God the smile of His approbation. That was truly a joyful meeting. Of all that company there is not one who has forgotten that day; nor will he forget it ever. With unreserved frankness they told Jesus of all that they had done, and what they had taught; of all their acts, and all their conversations. Would it not be better for us, if we cultivated more assiduously this habit of intimate intercourse with the Savior? Were we every day to tell Jesus of all that we have done and said; did we spread before Him our joys and our sorrows, our faults and our infirmities, our successes and our failures, we should be saved from many an error and many a sin. Setting the Lord always before us, He would be on our right hand, and we should not be moved. "He that dwelleth in the secret place of the most High shall abide under the shadow of the Almighty."

The Savior perceived that the apostles needed much instruction which could not be communicated in a place where both He and they were so well known. They had committed many errors, which He preferred to correct in private. By doing His will, they had learned to repose greater confidence in His wisdom, and were prepared to receive from Him more important instruction. But these lessons could not be delivered in the hearing of a promiscuous audience. Nor wasthis all. He perceived that the apostles were worn out with their labors, and needed repose. Surrounded as they were by the multitude, which had already begun to collect about them, rest and retirement were equally impossible. "There were many coming and going, and they had no leisure, even so much as to eat." He therefore said to them, "Come ye yourselves apart into a desert place, and rest a while." For this purpose, He "took ship, and crossed over with his disciples alone, and went into a desert place belonging to Bethsaida."

The religion of Christ imposes upon us duties of retirement, as well as duties of publicity. The apostles had been for some time past before the eyes of all men, preaching and working miracles. Their souls needed retirement. "Solitude," said Cecil, "is my great ordinance." They would be greatly improved by private communion both with Him and with each other. It was for the purpose of affording them such a season of moral recreation, that our Lord withdrew them from the public gaze into a desert place. Nor was this all. Their labor for some weeks past had been severe. They had traveled on foot under a tropical sun, reasoning with unbelievers, instructing the ignorant, and comforting the cast-down. Called upon, at all hours, both of the day and night, to work cures on those that were opprest with diseases, their bodies, no less than their spirits, needed rest. Our Lord saw this, and He made provision for it. He withdrew them from labor, that they might find, tho it were but for a day, the repose which their exhausted natures demanded. The religion of Christ is ever merciful, and ever consistent in its benevolence. It is thoughtful of the benefactor as well as the recipient. It requires of us all labor and self-sacrifice, but to these it affixes a limit. It never commands us to ruin our health and enfeeble our minds by unnatural exhaustion. It teaches us to obey the laws of our physical organization, and to prepare ourselves for the labors of to-morrow by the judiciously conducted labors of to-day. It was on this principle that our Lord conducted His intercourse with His disciples. "He knew their frame, and remembered that they were dust."

May we not from this incident derive a lesson of practical instruction? I well know that there are persons who are always sparing themselves, who, while it is difficult to tell what they do, are always complaining of the crushing weight of their labors, and who are rather exhausted with the dread of what they shall do, than with the experience of what they have actually done. It is not of those that we speak. Those who do not labor have no need of rest. It is to the honest, the painstaking, the laborious, that we address the example in the text. We sometimes meet with the industrious, self-denying servant of Christ, in feeble health, and with an exhausted nature, bemoaning his condition, and condemning himself because he can accomplish no more, while so much yet remains to be done. To such a one we may safely present the example of the blessed Savior. When His apostles had done to the utmost of their strength, altho the harvest was great, and the laborers few, He did not urge upon them additional labor, nor tell them that because there was so much to be done they must never cease from doing. No; He tells them to turn aside and rest for a while. It is as tho He had said, "Your strength is exhausted; you cannot be qualified for subsequent duty until you be refreshed. Economize, then, your power, that you may accomplish the more." The Savior addresses the same language to us now. When we are worn down in His service, as in any other, He would have us rest, not for the sake of self-indulgence, but that we may be the better prepared for future effort. We do nothing at variance with His will, when we, with a good conscience, use the liberty which he has thus conceded to us.

Jesus, with His disciples, crossed the water, and entered the desert; that is, the sparsely inhabited country of Bethsaida. Desert, or wilderness, in the New Testament, does not mean an arid waste, but pasture land, forest, or any district to which one could retire for seclusion. Here, in the cool and tranquil neighborhood of the lake, he began to instruct His disciples, and, without interruption, make known to them the mysteries of the kingdom. It was one of those seasons that the Savior Himself rarely enjoyed. Everything tended to repose: the rustling leaves, the rippling waves, the song of the birds, heard more distinctly in this rural solitude, all served to calm the spirit ruffled by the agitations of the world, and prepared it to listen to the truths which unveil to us eternity. Here our Lord could unbosom Himself, without reserve, to His chosen few, and hold with them that communion which He was rarely permitted to enjoy during His ministry on earth.

Soon, however, the whole scene is changed. The multitude, whom he had so recently left, having observed the direction in which He had gone, have discovered the place of His retreat. An immense crowd approaches, and the little company is surrounded by a dense mass of human beings pressing upon them on every side. These are, however, only the pioneers. At last, five thousand men, besides women and children, are beheld thronging around them.

Some of these suitors present most importunate claims. They are in search of cure for diseases which have baffled the skill of the medical profession, and, as a last resort, they have come to the Messiah for aid. Here was a parent bringing a consumptive child. There were children bearing on a couch a paralytic parent. Here was a sister leading a brother blind from his birth, while her supplications were drowned by the shout of a frenzied lunatic who was standing by her side. Every one, believing his own claim to be the most urgent, prest forward with selfish importunity. Each one, caring for no other than himself, was striving to attain the front rank, while those behind, disappointed, and fearing to lose this important opportunity, were eager to occupy the places of those more fortunate than themselves. The necessary tumult and disorder of such a scene you can better imagine than I can describe.

This was, doubtless, by no means a welcome interruption. The apostles needed the time for rest; for they were worn out in the public service. They wanted it for instruction; for such opportunities of intercourse with Christ were rare. But what did they do? Did our Lord inform the multitude that this day was set apart for their own refreshment and improvement, and that they could not be interrupted? As He beheld them approaching, did He quietly take to His boat, and leave them to go home disappointed? Did He plead His own convenience, or His need of repose, as any reason for not attending to the pressing necessities of His fellow men?

No, my brethren, very far from it. That providence of God had brought these multitudes before Him, and that same providence forbade Him to send them away unblest. He at once broke up the conference with His disciples and addrest Himself to the work before Him. His instructions were of inestimable importance; but I doubt if even they were as important as the example of deep humility, exhaustless kindness, and affecting compassion which He here exhibited. When the Master places work before us which can be done at no other time, our convenience must yield to other men's necessities. "The Son of Man came not to be ministered unto, but to minister." You can imagine to yourself the Savior rising from His seat, in the midst of His disciples, and presenting

Himself to the approaching multitudes. His calm dignity awes into silence this tumultuous gathering of the people. Those who came out to witness the tricks of an empiric, or listen to the ravings of a fanatic, find themselves, unexpectedly, in a presence that repels every emotion but that of profound veneration. The light-hearted and frivolous are awestruck by the unearthly majesty that seems to clothe the Messiah as with a garment. And yet it was a majesty that shone forth conspicuous, most of all, by the manifestation of unparalleled goodness. Every eye that met the eye of the Savior quailed before Him; for it looked into a soul that had never sinned; and the spirit of the sinner felt, for the first time, the full power of immaculate virtue.

Thus the Savior passed among the crowd, and "healed all that had need of healing." The lame walked, the lepers were cleansed, the blind received their sight, the paralytic were restored to soundness, and the bloom of health revisited the cheeks of those that but just now were sick unto death.

The work to be done for the bodies of men was accomplished, and there yet remained some hours of the summer's day unconsumed. The power and goodness displayed in this miraculous healing would naturally predispose the people to listen to the instructions of the Savior. This was too valuable an opportunity to be lost. Our Lord therefore proceeded to speak to them of the things concerning the kingdom of God. We can seem to perceive the Savior seeking an eminence from whence He could the more conveniently address this vast assembly. You hear Him unfold the laws of God's moral government. He unmasks the hypocrisy of the Pharisees; He rebukes the infidelity of the Sadducees; He exposes the folly of the frivolous, as well as of the selfish worldling; He speaks peaceably to the humble penitent; He encourages the meek, and comforts those that be cast down. The intellect and the conscience of this vast assembly are swayed at His will. The soul of man bows down in reverence in the presence of its Creator. "He stilleth the noise of the seas, the noise of their waves, and the tumult of the people." As He closes His address, every eye is moistened with compunction for sin. Every soul cherishes the hope of amendment. Every one is conscious that a new moral light has dawned upon his soul, and that a new moral universe has been unveiled to his spiritual vision. As the closing words of the Savior fell upon their ears, the whole multitude stood for a while unmoved, as tho transfixt to the earth by some mighty spell; until, at last, the murmur is heard from thousands of voices, "Never man spake like this man."

But the shades of evening are gathering around them. The multitude have nothing to eat. To send them away fasting would be inhuman, for divers of them came from far, and many were women and children, who could not perform their journey homeward without previous refreshment. To purchase food in the surrounding towns and villages would be difficult; but even were this possible, whence could the necessary funds be provided? A famishing multitude was thus unexpectedly cast upon the bounty of our Lord. He had not tempted God by leading them into the wilderness. They came to Him of themselves, to hear His words and to be healed of their infirmities. He could not "send them away fasting, lest they should faint by the way." In this dilemma, what was to be done? He puts this question to His disciples, and they can suggest no means of relief. The little stock of provisions which they had brought with them was barely sufficient for themselves. They can perceive no means whatever by which the multitude can be fed, and they at once confess it.

The Savior, however, commands the twelve to give them to eat. They produce their slender store of provisions, amounting to five loaves and two small fishes. He commands the multitude to sit down by companies on the grass. As soon as silence is obtained, He lifts up His eyes to heaven, and supplicates the blessing of God upon their scanty meal. He begins to break the loaves and fishes, and distribute them to His disciples, and His disciples distribute them to the multitude. He continues to break and distribute. Basket after basket is filled and emptied, yet the supply is undiminished. Food is carried in abundance to the famishing thousands. Company after company is supplied with food, but the five loaves and two fishes remain unexhausted. At last, the baskets are returned full, and it is announced that the wants of the multitude are supplied. The miracle then ceases, and the multiplication of food is at an end.

But even here the provident care of the Savior is manifested. Altho this food has been so easily provided, it is not right that it be lightly suffered to perish. Christ wrought no miracles for the sake of teaching men wastefulness. That food, by what means soever provided, was a creature of God, and it were sin to allow it to decay without accomplishing the purposes for which it was created. "Gather up the fragments," said the Master of the feast, "that nothing be lost." "And they gathered up the fragments that remained, twelve baskets full."

Dissimilar as are our circumstances to those of our Lord, we may learn from this latter incident a lesson of instruction.

In the first place, as I have remarked, the Savior did not lead the multitude into the wilderness without making provision for their sustenance. This would have been presumption. They followed Him without His command, and He found Himself with them in this necessity. He had provided for His own wants, but they had not provided for theirs. The providence of God had, however, placed Him in His present circumstances, and He might therefore properly look to providence for deliverance. This event, then, furnishes the rule by which we are to be governed. When we plunge ourselves into difficulty, by a neglect of the means or by a misuse of the faculties which God has bestowed upon us, it is to be expected that He will leave us to our own devices. But when, in the honest discharge of our duties, we find ourselves in circumstances beyond the reach of human aid, we may then confidently look up to God for deliverance. He will always take care of us while we are in the spot where He has placed us. When He appoints for us trials, He also appoints for us the means of escape. The path of duty, tho it may seem arduous, is ever the path of safety. We can more easily maintain ourselves in the most difficult position, God being our helper, than in apparent security relying on our own strength.

The Savior, in full reliance upon God, with only five loaves and two fishes, commenced the distribution of food amongst the vast multitude. Tho His whole store was barely sufficient to supply the wants of His immediate family, He began to share it with the thousands who surrounded Him. Small as was His provision at the commencement, it remained unconsumed until the deed of mercy was done, and the wants of the famished host supplied. Nor were the disciples losers by this act of charity. After the multitude had eaten and were satisfied, twelve baskets full of fragments remained, a reward for their deed of benevolence.

From this portion of the narrative, we may, I think, learn that if we act in faith, and in the spirit of Christian love, we may frequently be justified in commencing the most important good work, even when in possession of apparently inadequate means. If the work be of God, He will furnish us with helpers as fast as they are needed. In all ages, God has rewarded abundantly simple trust in Him, and has bestowed upon it in the highest honor. We must, however, remember the conditions upon which alone we may expect His aid, lest we be led into fanaticism. The service which we undertake must be such as God has commanded, and His providence must either designate us for the work, or, at least, open the door by which we shall enter upon it. It must be God's work, and not our own; for the good of others, and not for the gratification of our own passions; and, in the doing of it, we must, first of all, make sacrifice of ourselves, and not of others. Under such circumstances, there is hardly a good design which we may not undertake with cheerful hopes of success, for God has promised us His assistance. "If God be for us, who can be against us?" The calculations of the men of this world are of small account in such a matter. It would have provoked the smile of an infidel to behold the Savior commencing the work of feeding five thousand men with a handful of provisions. But the supply increased as fast as it was needed, and it ceased not until all that

He had prayed for was accomplished.

Perhaps, also, we may learn from this incident another lesson. If I mistake not, it suggests to us that in works of benevolence we are accustomed to rely too much on human, and too little on divine, aid. When we attempt to do good, we commence by forming large associations, and suppose that our success depends upon the number of men whom we can unite in the promotion of our undertaking. Every one is apt thus to forget his own personal duty, and rely upon the labor of others, and it is well if he does not put his organization in the place of God Himself. Would it not be better if we made benevolence much more a matter between God and our own souls, each one doing with his own hands, in firm reliance on divine aid, the work which Providence has placed directly before him? Our Lord did not send to the villages round to organize a general effort to relieve the famishing. In reliance upon God, He set about to work Himself, with just such means as God had afforded Him. All the miracles of benevolence have, if I mistake not, been wrought in the same manner. The little band of disciples in Jerusalem accomplished more for the conversion of the world than all the Christians of the present day united. And why? Because every individual Christian felt that the conversion of the world was a work for which he himself, and not an abstraction that he called the Church, was responsible. Instead of relying on man for aid, every one looked up directly to God, and went forth to the work. God was thus exalted, the power was confest to be His own, and, in a few years, the standard of the Cross was carried to the remotest extremities of the then known world.

Such has, I think, been the case ever since. Every great moral reformation has proceeded upon principles analogous of these. It was Luther, standing up alone in simple reliance upon God, that smote the Papal hierarchy; and the effects of that blow are now agitating the nations of Europe. Roger Williams, amid persecution and banishment, held forth that doctrine of soul-liberty which, in its onward march, is disenthralling a world.

Howard, alone, undertook the work of showing mercy to the prisoner, and his example is now enlisting the choicest minds in Christendom in this labor of benevolence. Clarkson, unaided, a young man, and without influences, consecrated himself to the work of abolishing the slave trade; and, before he rested from his labor, his country had repented of and forsaken this atrocious sin. Raikes saw the children of Gloucester profaning the Sabbath day; he set on foot a Sabbath school on his own account, and now millions of children are reaping the benefit of his labors, and his example has turned the attention of the whole world to the religious instruction of the young. With such facts before us, we surely should be encouraged to attempt individually the accomplishment of some good design, relying in humility and faith upon Him who is able to grant prosperity to the feeblest effort put forth in earnest reliance on His almightiness.

Such were the occupations that filled up a day in the life of Jesus of Nazareth. There was not an act done for Himself; all was done for others. Every hour was employed in the labor which that hour set before Him. Private kindness, the relief of distress, public teaching, and ministration to the wants of the famishing, filled up the entire day. Let His disciples learn to follow His example. Let us, like Him, forget ourselves, our own wants, and our own weariness, that we may, as he did, scatter blessings on every side, as we move onward in the pathway of our daily life. If such were the occupations of the Son of God, can we do more wisely than to imitate His example? Every disciple would then be as a city set upon a hill, and men, seeing our good works, would glorify our Father who is in heaven. "Then would our righteousness go forth as brightness, and our salvation as a lamp that burneth."

VINET

THE MYSTERIES OF CHRISTIANITY

BIOGRAPHICAL NOTE

Alexander Vinet, the eminent Swiss divine and author, was born at Ouchy, Canton, in 1797. He was professor of theology at Lausanne (1837-45), where he gained reputation as a preacher, a philosopher, and a writer. He was tolerant tho critical, and many of his utterances are marked by rare brilliancy. His supreme and intense faith led him to say: "The gospel is believed when it has ceased to be to us an external and has become an internal truth, when it has become a fact in our consciousness. Christianity is conscience raised to its highest exercise." He died in 1847.

VINET

1797-1847

THE MYSTERIES OF CHRISTIANITY

Things which have not entered into the heart of man.
—1 Cor. ii., 9.

"I do not comprehend, therefore I do not believe." "The gospel is full of mysteries, therefore I do not receive the gospel:"—such is one of the favorite arguments of infidelity. To see how much is made of this, and what confidence it inspires, we might believe it solid, or, at least, specious; but it is neither the one nor the other; it will not bear the slightest attention, the most superficial examination of reason; and if it still enjoys some favor in the world, this is but a proof of the lightness of our judgments upon things worthy of our most serious attention.

Upon what, in fact, does this argument rest? Upon the claim of comprehending every thing in the religion which God has offered or could offer us—a claim equally unjust, unreasonable, useless. This we proceed to develop.

1. In the first place, it is an unjust claim. It is to demand of God what He does not owe us. To prove this, let us suppose that God has given a religion to man, and let us further suppose that religion to be the gospel: for this absolutely changes nothing to the argument. We may believe that God was free, at least, with reference to us, to give us or not to give us a religion; but it must be admitted that in granting it He contracts engagements to us, and that the first favor lays Him under a necessity of conferring other favors. For this is merely to say that God must be consistent, and that He finishes what He has begun. Since it is by a written

133

revelation He manifests His designs respecting us, it is necessary He should fortify that revelation by all the authority which would at least determine us to receive it; it is necessary He should give us the means of judging whether the men who speak to us in His name are really sent by Him; in a word, it is necessary we should be assured that the Bible is truly the Word of God.

It would not indeed be necessary that the conviction of each of us should be gained by the same kind of evidence. Some shall be led to Christianity by the historical or external arguments; they shall prove to themselves the truth of the Bible as the truth of all history is proved; they shall satisfy themselves that the books of which it is composed are certainly those of the times and of the authors to which they are ascribed. This settled, they shall compare the prophecies contained in these ancient documents with the events that have happened in subsequent ages; they shall assure themselves of the reality of the miraculous facts related in these books, and shall thence infer the necessary intervention of divine power, which alone disposes the forces of nature, and can alone interrupt or modify their action. Others, less fitted for such investigations, shall be struck with the internal evidence of the Holy Scriptures. Finding there the state of their souls perfectly described, their wants fully exprest, and the true remedies for their maladies completely indicated; struck with a character of truth and candor which nothing can imitate; in fine, feeling themselves in their inner nature moved, changed, renovated, by the mysterious influence of these holy writings, they shall acquire, by such means, a conviction of which they can not always give an account to others, but which is not the less legitimate, irresistible, and immovable. Such is the double road by which an entrance is gained into the asylum of faith. But it was due from the wisdom of God, from His justice, and, we venture to say it, from the honor of His government, that He should open to man this double road; for, if He desired man to be saved by knowledge, on the same principle He engaged Himself to furnish him the means of knowledge.

Behold, whence come the obligations of the Deity with reference to us, which obligations He has fulfilled. Enter on this double method of proof. Interrogate history, time and places, respecting the authenticity of the Scriptures; grasp all the difficulties, sound all the objections; do not permit yourselves to be too easily convinced; be the more severe upon that book, as it professes to contain the sovereign rule of your life, and the disposal of your destiny; you are permitted to do this, nay, you are encouraged to do it, provided you proceed to the investigation with the requisite capacities and with pure intentions. Or, if you prefer another method, examine, with an honest heart, the contents of the Scriptures; inquire, while you run over the words of Jesus, if ever man spake like this Man; inquire if the wants of your soul, long deceived, and the anxieties of your spirit, long cherished in vain, do not, in the teaching and work of Christ, find that satisfaction and repose which no wisdom was ever able to procure you; breathe, if I may thus express myself, that perfume of truth, of candor and purity, which exhales from every page of the gospel; see, if, in all these respects, it does not bear the undeniable seal of inspiration and divinity. Finally, test it, and if the gospel produces upon you a contrary effect, return to the books and the wisdom of men, and ask of them what Christ has not been able to give you.

But if, neglecting these two ways, made accessible to you, and trodden by the feet of ages, you desire, before all, that the Christian religion should, in every point, render itself comprehensible to your mind, and complacently strip itself of all mysteries; if you wish to penetrate beyond the veil, to find there, not the aliment which gives life to the soul, but that which would gratify your restless curiosity, I maintain that you raise against God a claim the most indiscreet, the most rash and unjust; for He has never engaged, either tacitly or expressly, to discover to you the secret which your eye craves; and such audacious importunity is fit to excite His indignation. He has given you what He owed you, more indeed than He owed you; the rest is with Himself.

If a claim so unjust could be admitted, where, I ask you, would be the limit of your demands? Already you require more from God than He has accorded to angels; for these eternal mysteries which trouble you, the harmony of the divine prescience with human freedom, the origin of evil and its ineffable remedy, the incarnation of the eternal Word—the relations of the God-man with His Father—the atoning virtue of His sacrifice, the regenerating efficacy of the Spirit-comforter, all these things are secrets, the knowledge of which is hidden from angels themselves, who, according to the word of the Apostle, stoop to explore their depths, and can not.

If you reproach the Eternal for having kept the knowledge of these divine mysteries to Himself, why do you not reproach Him for the thousand other limits He has prescribed for you? Why not reproach Him for not having given you wings like a bird, to visit the regions, which, till now, have been scanned only by your eyes? Why not reproach Him for not giving you, besides the five senses with which you are provided, ten other senses which He has perhaps granted to other creatures, and which procure for them perceptions of which you have no idea? Why not, in fine, reproach Him for having caused the darkness of night to succeed the brightness of day invariably on the earth? Ah! you do not reproach Him for that. You love that night which brings rest to so many fatigued bodies and weary spirits; which suspends in so many wretches, the feeling of grief; that night, during which orphans, slaves, and criminals cease to be, because over all their misfortunes and sufferings it spreads, with the opiate of sleep, the thick veil of oblivion; you love that night which, peopling the deserts of the heavens with ten thousand stars, not known to the day, reveals the infinite to our ravished imagination.

Well, then, why do you not, for a similar reason, love the night of divine mysteries, night, gracious and salutary, in which reason humbles itself, and finds refreshment and repose; where the darkness even is a revelation; where one of the principal attributes of God, immensity, discovers itself much more fully to our mind; where, in fine, the tender relations He has permitted us to form with Himself, are guarded from all admixture of familiarity by the thought that the Being who has humbled Himself to us, is, at the same time, the inconceivable God who reigns before all time, who includes in Himself all existences and all conditions of existence, the center of all thought, the law of all law, the supreme and final reason of every thing! So that, if you are just, instead of reproaching Him for the secrets of religion, you will bless Him that He has enveloped you in mysteries.

2. But this claim is not only unjust toward God; it is also in itself exceedingly unreasonable.

What is religion? It is God putting Himself in communication with man; the Creator with the creature, the infinite with the finite. There already, without going further, is a mystery; a mystery common to all religions, impenetrable in all religions. If, then, every thing which is a mystery offends you, you are arrested on the threshold, I will not say of Christianity, but of every religion; I say, even of that religion which is called natural, because it rejects revelation and miracles; for it necessarily implies, at the very least, a connection, a communication of some sort between God and man—the contrary being equivalent to atheism. Your claim prevents you from having any belief; and because you have not been willing to be Christians, it will not allow you to be deists.

"It is of no consequence," you say, "we pass over that difficulty; we suppose between God and us connections we can not conceive; we admit them because they are necessary to us. But this is the only step we are willing to take: we have already yielded too much to yield more." Say more, say you have granted too much not to grant much more, not to grant all! You have consented to admit, without comprehending it, that there may be communications from God to you, and from you to God. But consider well what is implied in such a supposition. It implies that you are dependent, and yet free: this you do not comprehend; it implies that the Spirit of God can make itself understood by your spirit: this you

137

do not comprehend; it implies that your prayers may exert an influence on the will of God: this you do not comprehend. It is necessary you should receive all these mysteries, in order to establish with God connections the most vague and superficial, and by the very side of which atheism is placed. And when, by a powerful effort with yourselves you have done so much as to admit these mysteries, you recoil from those of Christianity! You have accepted the foundation, and refuse the superstructure! You have accepted the principle and refuse the details! You are right, no doubt, so soon as it is proved to you, that the religion which contains these mysteries does not come from God; or rather, that these mysteries contain contradictory ideas. But you are not justified in denying them, for the sole reason that you do not understand them; and the reception you have given to the first kind of mysteries compels you, by the same rule, to receive the others.

This is not all. Not only are mysteries an inseparable part, nay, the very substance of all religion, but it is absolutely impossible that a true religion should not present a great number of mysteries. If it is true, it ought to teach more truths respecting God and divine things than any other, than all others together; but each of these truths has a relation to the infinite, and by consequence borders on a mystery. How should it be otherwise in religion, when it is thus in nature itself? Behold God in nature! The more He gives us to contemplate, the more He gives to astonish us. To each creature is attached some mystery. A grain of sand is an abyss! Now, if the manifestations which God has made of Himself in nature suggest to the observer a thousand questions which can not be answered, how will it be, when to that first revelation, another is added; when God the Creator and Preserver reveals Himself under new aspects as God the Reconciler and Savior? Shall not mysteries multiply with discoveries? With each new day shall we not see associated a new night? And shall we not purchase each increase of knowledge with an increase of ignorance? Has not the doctrine of grace, so necessary, so consoling, alone opened a profound abyss, into which, for eighteen centuries, rash and restless spirits have been constantly plunging?

It is, then, clearly necessary that Christianity should, more than any other religion, be mysterious, simply because it is true. Like mountains, which, the higher they are, cast the larger shadows, the gospel is the more obscure and mysterious on account of its sublimity. After this, will you be indignant that you do not comprehend every thing in the gospel? It would, forsooth, be a truly surprising thing if the ocean could not be held in the hollow of your hand, or uncreated wisdom within the limits of your intelligence! It would be truly unfortunate if a finite being could not embrace the infinite, and that, in the vast assemblage of things there should be some idea beyond its grasp! In other words, it would be truly unfortunate if God Himself should know something which man does not know!

Let us acknowledge, then, how insensate is such a claim when it is made with reference to religion.

But let us also recollect how much, in making such a claim, we shall be in opposition to ourselves; for the submission we dislike in religion, we cherish in a thousand other things. It happens to us every day to admit things we do not understand, and to do so without the least repugnance. The things, the knowledge of which is refused us, are much more numerous than we perhaps think. Few diamonds are perfectly pure; still fewer truths are perfectly clear. The union of our soul with our body is a mystery—our most familiar emotions and affections are a mystery—the action of thought and of will is a mystery—our very existence is a mystery. Why do we admit these various facts? Is it because we understand them? No, certainly, but because they are self-evident, and because they are truths by which we live. In religion we have no other course to take. We ought to know whether it is true and necessary; and once convinced of these two points, we ought, like the angels, to submit to the necessity of being ignorant of some things. And why do we not submit cheerfully to a privation which, after all, is not one?

3. To desire the knowledge of mysteries is to desire what is utterly useless; it is to raise, as I have said before, a claim the most vain and idle. What in reference to us is the object of the gospel? Evidently to regenerate and save us. But it attains this end wholly by the things it reveals. Of what use would it be to know those it conceals from us? We possess the knowledge which can enlighten our consciences, rectify our inclinations, renew our hearts; what should we gain if we possest other knowledge? It infinitely concerns us to know that the Bible is the Word of God; does it equally concern us to know in what way the holy men that wrote it were moved by the Holy Ghost? It is of infinite moment to us to know that Jesus Christ is the Son of God; need we know precisely in what way the divine and human natures are united in His adorable person? It is of infinite importance for us to know that unless we are born again we can not enter the kingdom of God, and that the Holy Spirit is the author of the new birth; shall we be further advanced if we know the divine process by which that wonder is performed? Is it not enough for us to know the truths that save? Of what use, then, would it be to know those which have not the slightest bearing on our salvation? "Tho I know all mysteries," says St. Paul, "and have not charity, I am nothing." St. Paul was content not to know, provided he had charity; shall not we, following his example, be content also without knowledge, provided that, like him, we have charity, that is to say, life?

But some one will say "If the knowledge of mysteries is really without influence on our salvation, why have they been indicated to us at all?" What if it should be to teach us not to be too prodigal of our "wherefores!" if it should be to serve as an exercise of our faith, a test of our submission! But we will not stop with such a reply.

Observe, I pray you, in what manner the mysteries of which you complain have taken their part in religion. You readily perceive they are not by themselves, but associated with truths which have a direct bearing on your salvation. They contain them, they serve to develop them; but they are not themselves the truths that save. It is with these mysteries as it is with the vessel that contains a medicinal draft—it is not the vessel that cures, but the draft; yet the draft could not be presented without the vessel. Thus each truth that saves is contained in a mystery, which, in itself, has no power to save. So the great work of expiation is necessarily attached to the incarnation of the Son of God, which is a mystery; so the sanctifying graces of the new covenant are necessarily connected with the effluence of the Holy Spirit, which is a mystery; so, too, the divinity of religion finds a seal and an attestation in the miracles, which are mysteries. Everywhere the light is born from darkness, and darkness accompanies the light. These two orders of truths are so united, so interlinked, that you can not remove the one without the other, and each of the mysteries you attempt to tear from religionwould carry with it one of the truths which bear directly on your regeneration and salvation. Accept the mysteries, then, not as truths that can save you, but as the necessary conditions of the merciful work of the Lord in your behalf.

The true point at issue in reference to religion is this:—Does the religion which is proposed to us change the heart, unite to God, prepare for heaven? If Christianity produces these effects, we will leave the enemies of the cross free to revolt against its mysteries, and tax them with absurdity. The gospel, we will say to them, is then an absurdity; you have discovered it. But behold what a new species of absurdity that certainly is which attaches man to all his duties, regulates human life better than all the doctrines of sages, plants in his bosom harmony, order, and peace, causes him joyfully to fulfil all the offices of civil life, renders him better fitted to live, better fitted to die, and which, were it generally received, would be the support and safeguard of society! Cite to us, among all human absurdities, a single one which produces such effects. If that "foolishness" we preach produces effects like these, is it not natural to conclude that it is truth itself? And if these things have not entered the heart of man, it is not because they are absurd, but because they are divine.

Make but a single reflection. You are obliged to confess that none of the religions which man may invent can satisfy his wants, or save his soul. Thereupon you have a choice to make. You will either reject them all as insufficient and false, and seek for nothing better, since man can not invent better, and then you will abandon to chance, to caprice of temperament or of opinion, your moral life and future destiny; or you will adopt that other religion which some treat as folly, and it will render you holy and pure, blameless in the midst of a perverse generation, united to God by love, and to your brethren by charity, indefatigable in doing good, happy in life, happy in death. Suppose, after all this, you shall be told that this religion is false; but meanwhile, it has restored in you the image of God, reestablished your primitive connections with that great Being, and put you in a condition to enjoy life and the happiness of heaven. By means of it you have become such that at the last day, it is impossible that God should not receive you as His children and make you partakers of His glory. You are made fit for paradise, nay, paradise has commenced for you even here, because you love. This religion has done for you what all religions propose, and what no other has realized. Nevertheless, by the supposition, it is false! And what more could it do, were it true? Rather do you not see that this is a splendid proof of its truth? Do you not see that it is impossible that a religion which leads to God should not come from God, and that the absurdity is precisely that of supposing that you can be regenerated by a falsehood?

Suppose that afterward, as at the first, you do not comprehend. It seems necessary, then, you should be saved by the things you do not comprehend. Is that a misfortune? Are you the less saved? Does it become you to demand from God an explanation of an obscurity which does not injure you, when, with reference to every thing essential, He has been prodigal of light? The first disciples of Jesus, men without culture and learning, received truths which they did not comprehend, and spread them through the world. A crowd of sages and men of genius have received, from the hands of these poor people, truths which they comprehended no more than they. The ignorance of the one, and the science of the other, have been equally docile. Do, then, as the ignorant and the wise have done. Embrace with affection those truths which have never entered into your heart, and which will save you. Do not lose, in vain discussions, the time which is gliding away, and which is bearing you into the cheering or appalling light of eternity. Hasten to be saved. Love now; one day you will know. May the Lord Jesus prepare you for that period of light, of repose, and of happiness!

SUMMERFIELD

THE HEAVENLY INHERITANCE

BIOGRAPHICAL NOTE

John Summerfield was born in England in 1798, and came to New York in 1821, where he soon became one of the most popular and eloquent preachers of that day. He belonged to the Methodist Communion and his name is still perpetuated in the names of many Methodist churches. He was unusually simple and modest in his tastes and habits, but when he spoke from the pulpit he produced a great impression by the force and daring of his style. He gave promise of equaling Whitefield as a pulpit orator, but he was subject to delicate health and prematurely died in 1825, twenty-seven years of age.

SUMMERFIELD

1798-1825
THE HEAVENLY INHERITANCE

For so an entrance shall be ministered unto you abundantly into the everlasting kingdom of our Lord and Saviour Jesus Christ.
—2 Peter i., 11.

Of all the causes which may be adduced to account for the indifference which is so generally manifested toward those great concerns of eternity, in which men are so awfully interested, none appears to me so likely to resolve the mystery, as that unbelief which lies at the core of every heart, hindering repentance, and so making faith impossible. Men hear that there is a hell to shun, a heaven to win; and, though they give their assent to both these truths, they never impress them on their mind. It is plain that, whatever their lips may confess, they never believed with the heart, otherwise some effect would have been produced in the life. The germ of unbelief lies within, and discovers itself in all that indifference which is displayed, in the majority of that class of beings whose existence is to be perpetuated throughout eternity. If these thoughts do sometimes obtrude themselves on their serious attention, they are immediately banished from their minds; and the dying exclamation of Moses may be taken up with tears by every lover of perishing sinners: "O! that they were wise, that they understood this, that they would consider their latter end!" When God, by His prophet Isaiah, called the Israelites to a sense of their awful departure from Him, His language was, "My people do not know: My people do not consider." How few are there like Mary, who "ponder those things in their heart," who

147

are willing to look at themselves, to pry into eternity, to put the question home,

> "Shall I be with the damn'd cast out,Or numbered with the bless'd?"

This question must sooner or later have a place in your minds, or awful will be your state indeed; let it reach your hearts to-day; and if you pray to the Father of light, you will soon be enabled in His light to discern so much of yourselves as will cause you to cry, "What shall I do to be saved?" While we shall this morning attempt to point out some of the privileges of the sons of God, oh! may your hearts catch the strong desire to be conformed to the living Head, that so an abundant entrance may be administered unto you also, into the everlasting kingdom of our Lord and Savior, Jesus Christ.

The privilege to which our text leads us, is exclusively applicable to those to whom that question has been solved by the Spirit of God; those who have believed to the saving of their souls; who have experienced redemption through His blood, and the forgiveness of sins; and who are walking in the fear of the Lord and in the comfort of the Holy Ghost.

I. The state to which we look forward: the "everlasting kingdom of our Lord and Savior."

1. It is a kingdom. By this figurative expression our Lord has described the state of grace here and of glory hereafter; our happiness in time and our happiness in eternity. They were wisely so called: Jesus has said, as well as done, all things well; for these two states differ not in kind, but in degree; the one is merely a preparative for the other, and he who has been a subject of the former kingdom will be a subject of the latter. Grace is but the seed of glory, glory is the maturity of grace; grace is but the bud of glory, glory is grace full blown; grace is but the blossom of glory, glory is the ripe fruit of grace; grace is but the infant of glory, glory is the perfection of grace. Hence our hymn

beautifully says, "The men of grace have found glory begun below," agreeing with our Lord's own words, "He that believeth hath everlasting life"; he feels even here its glories beginning—a foretaste of its bliss.

Now the propriety with which these two states are called kingdoms is manifest from the analogy which might be traced between them and the model of a human sovereignty. Two or three of the outlines of this model will be sufficient.

In the idea of a kingdom it is implied that in some part of its extent there is the residence of a sovereign; for this is essential to constitute it. Now in the kingdom of grace the heart of the believer is made the residence of the King invisible! "Know ye not that your body is the temple of the Holy Ghost which is in you?" Such know what that promise means, "I will dwell in them, and they shall be my people." St. Paul exultingly cries, "Christ liveth in me."

Again, it is essential that the inhabitants of a kingdom be under the government of its laws. An empire without laws is no sovereignty at all; it ceases to be such, for every inhabitant has an equal right to do that which seems good in his own eyes. Now the subjects of Christ's kingdom of grace are "not without law, but are under a law to Christ"; they do His righteous will!

Lastly, it is essential that the subjects of a kingdom be under the protection of the presiding monarch, and that they repose their confidence in him. To the subjects of the kingdom of grace, Christ imparts His kingly protection; this is their heritage: "No weapon formed against them shall prosper"; nay, He imparts to them of His royal bounty, and they enjoy all the blessings of an inward heaven.

But how great the perfection of the kingdom of glory mentioned in our text! Does He make these vile bodies His residence here? How much more glorious is His temple above! how splendid the court of heaven! There, indeed, he fixes His throne, and they see Him as He is. Does He exercise His authority here and rule His happy subjects by the law, the perfect law of love? How much more in heaven! He reigns there forever over them; His government is there wholly by Himself; He knows nothing of a rival there; His rule is sole and perfect: there they serve Him day and night. Are His subjects here partakers of His kingly bounty? Much more in heaven! He calls them to a participation of all the joys, the spiritual joys which are at His right hand, and the pleasures which are there forevermore. Yet, after all our descriptions of that glory, it is not yet revealed, and, therefore, inconceivable. But who would not hail such a Son of David? who would not desire to be swayed by such a Prince of Peace? Whose heart would not ascend with the affections of our poet, "O! that with yonder sacred throng, we at His feet may fall"?

2. But it is an everlasting kingdom! Here it rises in the scale of comparison. Weigh the kingdoms of this world in this balance, and they are found wanting; for on many we read their fatal history, and ere long we shall see them all branded with the writing of the invisible Agent, "The kingdom is taken from thee, and given to a nation bringing forth the fruits thereof"; "For the kingdoms of this world have become the kingdoms of our Lord and of his Christ"; they will be absorbed and swallowed up in the fulness of eternity, and leave not a wrack behind! Every thing here is perishable! The towering diadem of Caesar has fallen from his head and crumbled into dust; and that kingdom whose scepter once swayed the world, betwixt whose colossal stride all nations were glad to creep to find themselves dishonored graves, is now forgotten, or, if its recollection be preserved, its history is emphatically called "The Decline and Fall."

But bring the matter nearer home; apply it not to multitudes of subjects, but to your individual experience, and has not that good teacher instructed you in this sad lesson? We tremble to look at our earthly possessions and employments, lest we should see them in motion, spreading their wings to fly away! How many are there already who, in talking of their comforts, are obliged to go back in their reckoning! Would not this be the language of some of you: "I had—I had a husband, the sharer of my joys, the soother of my sorrows; but he is not! I had a wife, a helpmeet for me; but where is she? I had children to whom I looked up as my support and staff in the decline of life, while passing down the hill; but I am bereaved of my children! I had health, and I highly prized its wealth; but now my emaciated frame, my shriveled system, and the pains of nature bespeak that comfort fled! I had, or fondly thought I had, happiness in possession! Then I said with Job, 'I shall die in my nest!' but ah! an unexpected blast passed over me, and now my joys are blighted! 'They have fled as a shadow, and continued not.'" Yes! time promised you much! perhaps it performed a little; but it can not do any thing for you on which it can grave "eternal." Its name is mortal, its nature is decay; it was born with man, and when the generations of men shall cease to exist, it will cease also: "Time shall be no longer!" We know concerning these that, "All flesh is as grass, and all the glory of man as the flower of grass. The grass withereth, and the flower fadeth, but the word of the Lord endureth forever." Yes! His kingdom is an everlasting kingdom; glory can not corrupt! the crown of glory can not fade! Why? Death will be destroyed; Christ will put this last enemy under His feet, and all will then be eternal life! Oh, happy, happy kingdom; nay, thrice happy he who shall be privileged to be its subject!

3. It is the everlasting kingdom of our own Lord and Savior Jesus Christ. It is His by claim: "Him hath God the Father highly exalted"; yea, Him hath He appointed to be "the judge of quick and dead"; for tho by the sufferings of death He was made a little lower than the angels, yet immediately after His resurrection He declares that now "All power is given unto him in heaven and in earth"! The Father hath committed all judgment unto the Son, and He has now the disposal of the offices and privileges of the empire among His faithful followers. This is the idea that the penitent dying thief had on the subject: "Lord, remember me when thou comest into thy kingdom"; and St. Paul expresses the same when he says to Timothy in the confidence of faith, "The Lord shall deliver me and preserve me unto his heavenly

kingdom." Oh! how pleasing the thought to the child of God, that his ruler to all eternity will be his elder Brother; for He who sanctifieth and they who are sanctified are all of one; and though He is heir of all things, yet we, as younger branches of the same heavenly family, shall be joint heirs, fellow-heirs of the same glorious inheritance. How great will be our joy to behold Him who humbled Himself for us to death, even the death of the cross, now exalted God over all, blest for evermore; and while contemplating Him under the character of our Lord and Savior Jesus Christ, how great the relish which will be given to that feeling of the redeemed which will constrain them to cry, "Thou alone art worthy to receive glory, and honor, and power."

II. But the apostle reminds us of the entrance into this kingdom!

1. The entrance into this kingdom is death: "By one man sin entered into the world, and death by sin:"

> "Death, like a narrow sea, dividesThat heavenly land from ours!"

"A messenger is sent to bring us to God, but it is the King of Terrors. We enter the land flowing with milk and honey, but it is through the valley of the shadow of death." Yet fear not, O thou child of God! there is no need that thou, through the fear of death, shouldst be all thy lifetime subject to bondage.

2. No; hear the apostle: the entrance is ministered unto thee! Death is but His minister; he can not lock his ice-cold hand in thine till He permit. Our Jesus has the keys of hell and death; and till He liberates the vassal to bring thee home, not a hair of thy head can fall to the ground! Fear not, thou worm! He who minds the sparrows appoints the time for thy removal: fear not; only be thou always ready, that, whenever the messenger comes to take down the tabernacle in which thy spirit has long made her abode, thou mayest be able to exclaim, "Amen! even so, Lord Jesus, come quickly." Death need have no terrors for thee; he is the vassal of thy Lord, and, however unwilling to do Him reverence, yet to

Him that sits at God's right hand shall even death pay, if not a joyful, yet a trembling homage; nay, more:

> "To Him shall earth and hell submit, And every foe shall fall, Till death expires beneath His feet, And God is all in all."

Christ has already had one triumph over death; His iron pangs could not detain the Prince who has "life in himself"; and in His strength thou shalt triumph, for the power of Christ is promised to rest upon thee! He has had the same entrance; His footsteps marked the way, and His cry to thee is, "Follow thou me." "My sheep," says He, "hear my voice, and they do follow me"; they follow Me gladly, even into this gloomy vale; and what is the consequence? "They shall never perish, neither shall any man pluck them out of my hand."

3. It is ministered unto you abundantly. Perhaps the apostle means that the death of some is distinguished by indulgences and honors not vouchsafed to all. In the experience of some, the passage appears difficult; in others it is comparatively easy; they gently fall asleep in Jesus. But we not only see diversities in the mortal agony—this would be a small thing.... Some get in with sails full spread and carrying a rich cargo indeed, while others arrive barely on a single plank. Some, who have long had their conversation in heaven, are anxious to be wafted into the celestial haven; while others, who never sought God till alarmed at the speedy approach of death, have little confidence,

> "And linger shivering on the brink, And fear to launch away."

This doctrine must have been peculiarly encouraging to the early converts to whom St. Peter wrote. From the tenor of both of his epistles it is clear that they were in a state of severe suffering, and in great danger of apostatizing through fear of persecution.

He reminds them that if they hold fast their professions, an abundant entrance will be administered unto them. The death of the martyr is far more glorious than that of the Christian who concealed his profession through fear of man. Witness the case of Stephen: he was not ashamed of being a witness for Jesus in the face of the violent death which awaited him, and which crushed the tabernacle of his devoted spirit; his Lord reserved the highest display of His love and of His glory for that awful hour! "Behold!" says he to his enemies, while gnashing on him with their teeth, "Behold! I see heaven opened, and the Son of man standing on the right hand of God"; then, in the full triumph of faith, he cries out, "Lord Jesus! receive my spirit!"

But did these things apply merely to the believers to whom St. Peter originally wrote? No; you are the men to whom they equally apply; according to your walk and profession of that gospel will be the entrance which will be ministered unto you. Some of you have heard, in another of our houses, during the past week, the dangerous tendency of the spirit of fear, the fear of man. I would you had all heard that discourse: alas! many who have a name and a place among us are becoming mere Sabbath-day worshipers in the courts of the Lord, and lightly esteem the daily means of grace. I believe this is one cause at least why many are weak and sickly among us in divine things. The inner man does not make due increase; the world is stealing a march unawares upon us. May God revive among us the spirit of our fathers!

These things, then, I say, equally apply to you. Behold the strait, the royal, the king's highway! Are you afraid of the reproach of Christ?

"Ashamed of Jesus, that dear Friend,On whom our hopes of heaven depend?"

How soon would the world be overcome if all who profess that faith were faithful to it! Wo to the rebellious children who compromise truth with the world, and in effect deny their Lord and Master! Who hath required this at their hands? Do they not follow with the crowd who cry, "Lord, Lord! and yet do not the things which He says"? Will they have the adoption and the glory? Will they aim at the honor implied in these words, "Ye are my witnesses?" Will ye indeed be sons? Then see the path wherein His footsteps shine! The way is open! see that ye walk therein! The false apostles, the deceitful workers shall have their reward; the same that those of old had, the praise and esteem of men; while the faith of those who truly call Him Father and Lord, and who walk in the light as He is in the light, who submit, like Him and His true followers, to be counted as "the filth of the world, and the offscouring of all things", shall be found unto praise, and honor, and glory!

The true Christian does not seek to hide himself in a corner; he lets his light shine before men, whether they will receive it or not; and thereby is his Father glorified. Having thus served, by the will of God, the hour of his departure at length arrives. The angels beckon him away; Jesus bids him come; and as he departs this life he looks back with a heavenly smile on surviving friends, and is enabled to say, "Whither I go, ye know, and the way ye know." An entrance is ministered unto him abundantly into the everlasting kingdom of his Lord and Savior.

III. Having considered the state to which we look, and the mode of our admission, let us consider the condition of it. This is implied in the word "so." "For so an entrance shall be ministered unto you." In the preceding part of this chapter, the apostle has pointed out the meaning of this expression, and in the text merely sums it all up in that short mode of expression.

The first condition he shows to be, the obtaining like precious faith with him, through the righteousness of God and our Savior Jesus Christ. Not a faith which merely assents to the truths of the gospel record, but a faith which applies the merits of the death of Christ to expiate my individual guilt; which lays hold on Him as my sacrifice, and produces, in its exercises, peace with God, a knowledge of the divine favor, a sense of sin forgiven, and a full certainty, arising from a divine impression on the heart, made by the Spirit of God, that I am accepted in the Beloved and made a child of God.

If those who profess the Gospel of Christ were but half as zealous in seeking after this enjoyment as they are in discovering creaturely objections to its attainment, it would be enjoyed by thousands who at present know nothing of its happy reality. Such persons, unfortunately for themselves, employ much more assiduity in searching a vocabulary to find out epithets of reproach to attach to those who maintain the doctrine than in searching that volume which declares that "if you are sons, God has sent forth the Spirit of his Son into your hearts, crying Abba, Father"; and that "he that believeth hath the witness in himself." In whatever light a scorner may view this doctrine now, the time will come when, being found without the wedding garment, he will be cast into outer darkness.

O sinner! cry to God this day to convince thee of thy need of this salvation, and then thou wilt be in a condition to receive it:

> "Shalt know, shalt feel thy sins forgiven,Bless'd with this antepast of heaven."

But, besides this, the apostle requires that we then henceforth preserve consciences void of offense toward God and toward man. This faith which obtains the forgiveness of sin unites to Christ, and by this union we are made, as St. Peter declares, "partakers of the divine nature": and as He who has called you is holy, so you are to be holy in all manner of conversation. For yours is a faith which not only casts out sin, but purifies the heart—the conscience having been once purged by the sprinkling of the blood of Christ, you are not to suffer guilt to be again contracted; for the salvation of Christ is not only from the penalty, but from the very stain of sin; not only from its guilt, but from its pollution; not only from its condemnation, but from its very "in-being"; "The blood of Jesus Christ cleanseth from all sin"; and

"For this purpose was the Son of God manifested, that he might destroy the works of the devil." You are therefore required by St. Peter, "to escape the corruption that is in the world through lust," and thus to perfect holiness in the fear of the Lord!

Finally, live in progressive and practical godliness. Not only possess, but practise, the virtues of religion; not only practise, but increase therein, abounding in the work of the Lord! Lead up, hand in hand, in the same delightful chorus, all the graces which adorn the Christian character. Having the divine nature, possessing a new and living principle, let diligent exercise reduce it to practical holiness; and you will be easily discerned from those formal hypocrites, whose faith and religion are but a barren and unfruitful speculation.

To conclude: live to God—live for God—live in God; and let your moderation be known unto all men—the Lord is at hand: "Therefore giving all diligence, add to your faith virtue; and to virtue, knowledge; and to knowledge, temperance; and to temperance, patience; and to patience, godliness; and to godliness, brotherly kindness; and to brotherly kindness, charity."

NEWMAN

GOD'S WILL THE END OF LIFE

BIOGRAPHICAL NOTE

John Henry Newman was born in London in 1801. He won high honors at Oxford, and in 1828 was appointed vicar of the University Church, St. Mary's, and with Keble and Pusey headed the Oxford Movement. In the pulpit of St. Mary's he soon showed himself to be a power. His sermons, exquisite, tho simple in style, chiefly deal with various phases of personal religion which he illustrated with a keen spiritual insight, a sympathetic glow, an exalted earnestness and a breadth of range, unparalleled in English pulpit utterances before his time. His extreme views on questions of catholicity, sacerdotalism and the sacraments, as well as his craving for an infallible authority in matters of faith, shook his confidence in the Church of England and he went over to Rome in 1845. He was made Cardinal in 1879 and died in 1890.

NEWMAN

1801-1890
GOD'S WILL THE END OF LIFE

I came down from heaven not to do mine own will but the will of him that sent me.—John vi., 38.

I am going to ask you a question, my dear brethren, so trite, and therefore so uninteresting at first sight, that you may wonder why I put it, and may object that it will be difficult to fix the mind on it, and may anticipate that nothing profitable can be made of it. It is this: "Why were you sent into the world?" Yet, after all, it is perhaps a thought more obvious than it is common, more easy than it is familiar; I mean it ought to come into your minds, but it does not, and you never had more than a distant acquaintance with it, tho that sort of acquaintance with it you have had for many years. Nay, once or twice, perhaps you have been thrown across the thought somewhat intimately, for a short season, but this was an accident which did not last. There are those who recollect the first time, as it would seem, when it came home to them. They were but little children, and they were by themselves, and they spontaneously asked themselves, or rather God spake in them, "Why am I here? how came I here? who brought me here? What am I to do here?" Perhaps it was the first act of reason, the beginning of their real responsibility, the commencement of their trial; perhaps from that day they may date their capacity, their awful power, of choosing between good and evil, and of committing mortal sin. And so, as life goes on, the thought comes vividly, from time to time, for a short season across their conscience; whether in illness, or in some anxiety,

161

or at some season of solitude, or on hearing some preacher, or reading some religious work. A vivid feeling comes over them of the vanity and unprofitableness of the world, and then the question recurs, "Why then am I sent into it?"

And a great contrast indeed does this vain, unprofitable, yet overbearing world present with such a question as that. It seems out of place to ask such a question in so magnificent, so imposing a presence, as that of the great Babylon. The world professes to supply all that we need, as if we were sent into it for the sake of being sent here, and for nothing beyond the sending. It is a great favor to have an introduction to this august world. This is to be our exposition, forsooth, of the mystery of life. Every man is doing his own will here, seeking his own pleasure, pursuing his own ends; that is why he was brought into existence. Go abroad into the streets of the populous city, contemplate the continuous outpouring there of human energy, and the countless varieties of human character, and be satisfied! The ways are thronged, carriage-way and pavement; multitudes are hurrying to and fro, each on his own errand, or are loitering about from listlessness, or from want of work, or have come forth into the public concourse, to see and to be seen, for amusement or for display, or on the excuse of business. The carriages of the wealthy mingle with the slow wains laden with provisions or merchandise, the productions of art or the demands of luxury. The streets are lined with shops, open and gay, inviting customers, and widen now and then into some spacious square or place, with lofty masses of brickwork or of stone, gleaming in the fitful sunbeam, and surrounded or fronted with what simulates a garden's foliage. Follow them in another direction, and you find the whole groundstead covered with large buildings, planted thickly up and down, the homes of the mechanical arts. The air is filled, below, with a ceaseless, importunate, monotonous din, which penetrates even to your innermost chamber, and rings in your ears even when you are not conscious of it; and overhead, with a canopy of smoke, shrouding God's day from the realms of obstinate, sullen toil. This is the end of man!

Or stay at home, and take up one of those daily prints, which are so true a picture of the world; look down the columns of advertisements, and you will see the catalog of pursuits, projects, aims, anxieties, amusements, indulgences which occupy the mind of man. He plays many parts: here he has goods to sell, there he wants employment; there again he seeks to borrow money, here he offers you houses, great seats or small tenements; he has food for the million, and luxuries for the wealthy, and sovereign medicines for the credulous, and books, new and cheap, for the inquisitive. Pass on to the news of the day, and you will learn what great men are doing at home and abroad: you will read of wars and rumors of wars; of debates in the legislature; of rising men, and old statesmen going off the scene; of political contests in this city or that country; of the collision of rival interests. You will read of the money market, and the provision market, and the market for metals; of the state of trade, the call for manufactures, news of ships arrived in port, of accidents at sea, of exports and imports, of gains and losses, of frauds and their detection. Go forward, and you arrive at discoveries in art and science, discoveries (so-called) in religion, the court and royalty, the entertainments of the great, places of amusement, strange trials, offenses, accidents, escapes, exploits, experiments, contests, ventures. Oh, this curious restless, clamorous, panting being, which we call life!—and is there to be no end to all this? Is there no object in it? It never has an end, it is forsooth its own object!

And now, once more, my brethren, put aside what you see and what you read of the world, and try to penetrate into the hearts, and to reach the ideas and the feelings of those who constitute it; look into them as closely as you can; enter into their houses and private rooms; strike at random through the streets and lanes: take as they come, palace and hovel, office or factory, and what will you find? Listen to their words, witness, alas! their works; you will find in the main the same lawless thoughts, the same unrestrained desires, the same ungoverned passions, the same earthly opinions, the same wilful deeds, in high and low, learned and unlearned; you will find them all to be living for the sake of living; they one and all seem to tell you, "We are our own center, our own end." Why are they toiling? why are they scheming? for what are they living? "We live to please ourselves; life is worthless except we have our own way; we are not sent here at all, but we find ourselves here, and we are but slaves unless we can think what we will, believe what we will, love what we will, hate what we will, do what we will. We detest interference on the part of God or man. We do not bargain to be rich or to be great; but we do bargain, whether rich or poor, high or low, to live for ourselves, to live for the lust of the moment, or, according to the doctrine of the hour, thinking of the future and the unseen just as much or as little as we please."

Oh, my brethren, is it not a shocking thought, but who can deny its truth? The multitude of men are living without any aim beyond this visible scene; they may from time to time use religious words, or they may profess a communion or a worship, as a matter of course, or of expedience, or of duty, but, if there was sincerity in such profession, the course of the world could not run as it does. What a contrast is all this to the end of life, as it is set before us in our most holy faith! If there was one among the sons of men, who might allowably have taken his pleasure, and have done his own will here below, surely it was He who came down on earth from the bosom of the Father, and who was so pure and spotless in that human nature which He put on Him, that He could have no human purpose or aim inconsistent with the will of His Father. Yet He, the Son of God, the Eternal Word, came, not to do His own will, but His who sent Him, as you know very well is told us again and again in Scripture. Thus the Prophet in the Psalter, speaking in His person, says, "Lo, I come to do thy will, O God." And He says in the Prophet Isaiah, "The Lord God hath opened mine ear, and I do not resist; I have not gone back." And in the gospel, when He hath come on earth, "My food is to do the will of him that sent me, and to finish his work." Hence, too, in His agony, He cried out, "Not my will, but thine, be done;" and St. Paul, in like manner, says, that "Christ pleased not himself;" and elsewhere, that, "tho he was God's Son, yet learned he obedience by the things which he suffered." Surely so it was; as being indeed the eternal coequal Son, His will was one and the same with the Father's will, and He had no submission of will to make; but He chose to take on Him man's nature and the will of that nature; he chose to take on Him affections, feelings, and inclinations proper to man, a will innocent indeed and good, but still a man's will, distinct from God's will; a will, which, had it acted simply according to what was pleasing to its nature, would, when pain and toil were to be endured, have held back from an active cooperation with the will of God. But, tho He took on Himself the nature of man, He took not on Him that selfishness, with which fallen man wraps himself round, but in all things He devoted Himself as a ready sacrifice to His Father. He came on earth, not to take His pleasure, not to follow His taste, not for the mere exercise of human affection, but simply to glorify His Father and to do His will. He came charged with a mission, deputed for a work; He looked not to the right nor to the left, He thought not of Himself, He offered Himself up to God.

Hence it is that He was carried in the womb of a poor woman, who, before His birth, had two journeys to make, of love and of obedience, to the mountains and to Bethlehem. He was born in a stable, and laid in a manger. He was hurried off to Egypt to sojourn there; then He lived till He was thirty years of age in a poor way, by a rough trade, in a small house, in a despised town. Then, when He went out to preach, He had not where to lay His head; He wandered up and down the country, as a stranger upon earth. He was driven out into the wilderness, and dwelt among the wild beasts. He endured heat and cold, hunger and weariness, reproach and calumny. His food was coarse bread, and fish from the lake, or depended on the hospitality of strangers. And as He had already left His Father's greatness on high, and had chosen an earthly home; so again, at that Father's bidding, He gave up the sole solace given Him in this world, and denied Himself His mother's presence. He parted with her who bore Him; He endured to be strange to her; He endured to call her coldly "woman," who was His own undefiled one, all beautiful, all gracious, the best creature of His hands, and the sweet nurse of His infancy. He put her aside, as Levi, His type, merited the sacred ministry, by saying to His parents and kinsmen, "I know you not." He exemplified in His own person the severe maxim, which He gave to His disciples, "He that loveth more than me is not worthy of me." In all these many ways He sacrificed every wish of His own; that we might understand, that, if He, the Creator, came into His world, not for His own pleasure, but to do His Father's will, we too have most surely some work to do, and have seriously to bethink ourselves what that work is.

Yes, so it is; realize it, my brethren;—every one who breathes, high and low, educated and ignorant, young and old, man and woman, has a mission, has a work. We are not sent into this world for nothing; we are not born at random; we are not here, that we may go to bed at night, and get up in the morning, toil for our bread, eat and drink, laugh and joke, sin when we have a mind, and reform when we are tired of sinning, rear a family and die. God sees every one of us; He creates every soul, He lodges it in the body, one by one, for a purpose. He needs, He deigns to need, every one of us. He has an end for each of us; we are all equal in His sight, and we are placed in our different ranks and stations, not to get what we can out of them for ourselves, but to labor in them for Him. As Christ had His work, we too have ours; as He rejoiced to do His work, we must rejoice in ours also.

St. Paul on one occasion speaks of the world as a scene in a theater. Consider what is meant by this. You know, actors on a stage are on an equality with each other really, but for the occasion they assume a difference of character; some are high, some are low, some are merry, and some sad. Well, would it not be simple absurdity in any actor to pride himself on his mock diadem, or his edgeless sword, instead of attending to his part? What, if he did but gaze at himself and his dress? what, if he secreted, or turned to his own use, what was valuable in it? Is it not his business, and nothing else, to act his part well? Common sense tells us so. Now we are all but actors in this world; we are one and all equal, we shall be judged as equals as soon as life is over; yet, equal and similar in ourselves, each has his special part at present, each has his work, each has his mission,—not to indulge his passions, not to make money, not to get a name in the world, not to save himself trouble, not to follow his bent, not to be selfish and self-willed, but to do what God puts on him to do.

Look at the poor profligate in the gospel, look at Dives; do you think he understood that his wealth was to be spent, not on himself, but for the glory of God?—yet forgetting this, he was lost for ever and ever. I will tell you what he thought, and how he viewed things: he was a young man, and had succeeded to a good estate, and he determined to enjoy himself. It did not strike him that his wealth had any other use than that of enabling him to take his pleasure. Lazarus lay at his gate; he might have relieved Lazarus; that was God's will; but he managed to put conscience aside, and he persuaded himself he should be a fool, if he did not make the most of this world, while he had the means. So he resolved to have his fill of pleasure; and feasting was to his mind a principal part of it. "He fared sumptuously every day"; everything belonging to him was in the best style, as men speak; his house, his furniture, his plate of silver and gold, his attendants, his establishments. Everything was for enjoyment, and for show, too; to attract the eyes of the world, and to gain the applause and admiration of his equals, who were the companions of his sins. These companions were doubtless such as became a person of such pretensions; they were fashionable men; a collection of refined, high-bred, haughty men, eating, not gluttonously, but what was rare and costly; delicate, exact, fastidious in their taste, from their very habits of indulgence; not eating for the mere sake of eating, or drinking for the mere sake of drinking, but making a sort of science of their sensuality; sensual, carnal, as flesh and blood can be, with eyes, ears, tongue steeped in impurity, every thought, look, and sense, witnessing or ministering to the evil one who ruled them; yet, with exquisite correctness of idea and judgment, laying down rules for sinning;—heartless and selfish, high, punctilious, and disdainful in their outward deportment, and shrinking from Lazarus, who lay at the gate, as an eye-sore, who ought for the sake of decency to be put out of the way. Dives was one of such, and so he lived his short span, thinking of nothing but himself, till one day he got into a fatal quarrel with one of his godless associates, or he caught some bad illness; and then he lay helpless on his bed of pain, cursing fortune and his physician that he was no better, and impatient that he was thus kept from enjoying his youth, trying to fancy himself mending when he was getting worse, and disgusted at those who would not throw him some word of comfort in his suspense, and turning more resolutely from his Creator in proportion to his suffering;— and then at last his day came, and he died, and (oh! miserable!) "was buried in hell." And so ended he and his mission.

This was the fate of your pattern and idol, oh, ye, if any of you be present, young men, who, tho not possest of wealth and rank, yet affect the fashions of those who have them. You, my brethren, have not been born splendidly, or nobly; you have not been brought up in the seats of liberal education; you have no high connections; you have not learned the manners nor caught the tone of good society; you have no share of the largeness of mind, the candor, the romantic sense of honor, the correctness of taste, the consideration for others, and the gentleness which the world puts forth as its highest type of excellence; you have not come near the courts of the mansions of the great; yet you ape the sin of Dives, while you are strangers to his refinement. You think it the sign of a gentleman to set yourselves above religion; to criticize the religious and professors of religion; to look at Catholic and Methodist with impartial contempt; to gain a smattering of knowledge on a number of subjects; to dip into a number of frivolous publications, if they are popular; to have read the latest novel; to have heard the singer and seen the actor of the day; to be well up with the news; to know the names and, if so be, the persons of public men, to be able to bow to them; to walk up and down the street with your heads on high, and to stare at whatever meets you; and to say and do worse things, of which these outward extravagances are but the symbol. And this is what you conceive you have come upon the earth for! The Creator made you, it seems, oh, my children, for this work and office, to be a bad imitation of polished ungodliness, to be a piece of tawdry and faded finery, or a scent which has lost its freshness, and does not but offend the sense! O! that you could see how absurd and base are such pretenses in the eyes of any but yourselves! No calling of life but is honorable; no one is ridiculous who acts suitably to his calling and estate; no one, who has good sense and humility, but may, in any state of life, be truly well-bred and refined; but ostentation, affectation, and ambitious efforts are, in every station of life, high or low, nothing but vulgarities. Put them aside, despise them yourselves. Oh, my very dear sons, whom I love, and whom I would fain serve;—oh, that you could feel that you have souls! oh, that you would have mercy on your souls! oh, that, before it is too late, you would betake yourselves to Him who is the source of all that is truly high and magnificent and beautiful, all that is bright and pleasant and secure what you ignorantly seek, in Him whom you so wilfully, so awfully despise!

He, alone, the Son of God, "the brightness of the Eternal Light, and the spotless mirror of His Majesty," is the source of all good and all happiness to rich and poor, high and low. If you were ever so high, you would need Him; if you were ever so low, you could offend Him. The poor can offend Him; the poor man can neglect his divinely appointed mission as well as the rich. Do not suppose, my brethren, that what I have said against the upper or the middle class will not, if you happen to be poor, also lie against you. Though a man were as poor as Lazarus, he could be as guilty as Dives. If you were resolved to degrade yourselves to the brutes of the field, who have no reason and no conscience, you need not wealth or rank to enable you to do so. Brutes have no wealth; they have no pride of life; they have no purple and fine linen, no splendid table, no retinue of servants, and yet they are brutes. They are brutes by the law of their nature; they are the poorest among the poor; there is not a vagrant and outcast who is so poor as they; they differ from him, not in their possessions, but in their want of a soul, in that he has a mission and they have not, he can sin and they can not. Oh, my brethren, it stands to reason, a man may intoxicate himself with a cheap draft, as well as with a costly one; he may steal another's money for his appetites, though he does not waste his own upon them; he may break through the natural and social laws which encircle him, and profane the sanctity of family duties, tho he be not a child of nobles, but a peasant or artisan,—nay, and perhaps he does so more frequently than they. This is not the poor's blessedness, that he has less temptations to self-indulgence, for he has as many, but that from his circumstances he receives the penances and corrections of self-indulgence. Poverty is the mother of many pains and sorrows in their season, and these are God's messengers to lead the soul to repentance; but, alas! if the poor man indulges his passions, thinks little of religion, puts off repentance, refuses to make an effort, and dies without conversion, it matters nothing that he was poor in this world, it matters nothing that he was less daring than the rich, it matters not that he promised himself God's favor, that he sent for the priest when death came, and received the last sacraments; Lazarus too, in that case, shall be buried with Dives in hell, and shall have had his consolation neither in this world nor in the world to come.

My brethren, the simple question is, whatever a man's rank in life may be, does he in that rank perform the work which God has given him to do? Now then, let me turn to others, of a very different description, and let me hear what they will say, when the question is asked them. Why, they will parry it thus: "You give us no alternative," they will say to me, "except that of being sinners or saints. You put before us our Lord's pattern, and you spread before us the guilt and ruin of the deliberate transgressor; whereas we have no intention of going so far one way or the other; we do not aim at being saints, but we have no desire at all to be sinners. We neither intend to disobey God's will, nor to give up our own. Surely there is a middle way, and a safe one, in which God's will and our will may both be satisfied. We mean to enjoy both this world and the next. We will guard against mortal sin; we are not obliged to guard against venial; indeed it would be endless to attempt it. None but saints do so; it is the work of a life; we need have nothing else to do. We are not monks, we are in the world, we are in business, we are parents, we have families; we must live for the day. It is a consolation to keep from mortal sin; that we do, and it is enough for salvation. It is a great thing to keep in God's favor; what indeed can we desire more? We come at due time to the sacraments; this is our comfort and our stay; did we die, we should die in grace, and escape the doom of the wicked. But if we once attempted to go further, where should we stop? how will you draw the line for us? The line between mortal and venial sin is very distinct; we understand that; but do you not see that, if we attended to our venial sins, there would be just as much reason to attend to one as to another? If we began to repress our anger, why not also repress vainglory? Why not also guard against niggardliness? Why not also keep from falsehood, from gossiping, from idling, from excess in eating? And, after all, without venial sin we never can be, unless indeed we have the prerogative of the Mother of God, which it would be almost heresy to ascribe to any one but her. You are not asking us to be converted; that we understand; we are converted, we were converted a long time ago. You bid us aim at an indefinite vague something, which is less than perfection, yet more than obedience, and which, without resulting in any tangible advantage, debars us from the pleasures and embarrasses us in the duties of this world."

This is what you will say; but your premises, my brethren, are better than your reasoning, and your conclusions will not stand. You have a right view why God has sent you into the world; viz., in order that you may get to heaven; it is quite true also that you would fare well indeed if you found yourselves there, you could desire nothing better; nor, it is true, can you live any time without venial sin. It is true also that you are not obliged to aim at being saints; it is no sin not to aim at perfection. So much is true and to the purpose; but it does not follow from it that you, with such views and feelings as you have exprest, are using sufficient exertions even for attaining purgatory. Has your religion any difficulty in it, or is it in all respects easy to you? Are you simply taking your own pleasure in your mode of living, or do you find your pleasure in submitting yourself to God's pleasure? In a word, is your religion a work? For if it be not, it is not religion at all. Here at once, before going into your argument, is a proof that it is an unsound one, because it brings you to the conclusion that, whereas Christ came to do a work, and all saints, nay, nay, and sinners to do a work too, you, on the contrary, have no work to do, because, forsooth, you are neither sinners nor saints; or, if you once had a work, at least that you have despatched it already, and you have nothing upon your hands. You have attained your salvation, it seems, before your time, and have nothing to occupy you, and are detained on earth too long. The work days are over, and your perpetual holiday is begun. Did then God send you, above all other men, into the world to be idle in spiritual matters? Is it your mission only to find pleasure in this world, in which you are but as pilgrims and sojourners? Are you more than sons of Adam, who, by the sweat of their brow, are to eat bread till they return to the earth out of which they are taken? Unless you have some work in hand, unless you are struggling, unless you are fighting with yourselves, you are no followers of those who "through many tribulations entered into the kingdom of God." A fight is the very token of a Christian. He is a soldier of Christ; high or low, he is this and nothing else. If you have triumphed over all mortal sin, as you seem to think, then you must attack your venial sins; there is no help for it; there is nothing else to do, if you would be soldiers of Jesus Christ. But, oh, simple souls! to think you have gained any triumph at all! No; you cannot safely be at peace with any, even the least malignant, of the foes of God; if you are at peace with venial sins, be certain that in their company and under their shadow mortal sins are lurking. Mortal sins are the children of venial, which, tho they be not deadly themselves, yet are prolific of death. You may think that you have killed the giants who had possession of your hearts, and that you have nothing to fear, but may sit at rest under your vine and under your fig-tree; but the giants will live again, they will rise from the dust, and, before you know where you are, you will be taken captive and slaughtered by the fierce, powerful, and eternal enemies of God.

The end of a thing is the test. It was our Lord's rejoicing in His last solemn hour, that He had done the work for which He was sent. "I have glorified thee on earth." He says in His prayer, "I have finished the work which thou gavest me to do; I have manifested thy name to the men whom thou hast given me out of the world." It was St. Paul's consolation also, "I have fought the good fight, I have finished the course, I have kept the faith; henceforth there is laid up for me a crown of justice, which the Lord shall render to me in that day, the just judge." Alas! alas! how different will be our view of things when we come to die, or when we have passed into eternity, from the dreams and pretenses with which we beguile ourselves now! What will Babel do for us then? Will it rescue our souls from the purgatory or the hell to which it sends them? If we were created, it was that we might serve God; if we have His gifts, it is that we may glorify Him; if we have a conscience, it is that we may obey it; if we have the prospect of heaven, it is that we may keep it before us; if we have light, that we may follow it, if we have grace, that we may save ourselves by means of it. Alas! alas! for those who die without fulfilling their mission; who were called to be holy, and lived in sin; who were called to worship Christ, and who plunged into this giddy and unbelieving world; who were called to fight, and who remained idle; who were called to be Catholics, and who did but remain in the religion of their birth! Alas for those who have had gifts and talent, and have not used, or have misused, or abused them; who have had wealth, and have spent it on themselves; who have had abilities, and have advocated what was sinful, or ridiculed what was true, or scattered doubts against what was sacred; who have had leisure, and have wasted it on wicked companions, or evil books, or foolish amusements! Alas! for those of whom the best can be said is, that they are harmless and naturally blameless, while they never have attempted to cleanse their hearts or to live in God's sight!

The world goes on from age to age, but the Holy Angels and Blessed Saints are always crying Alas, alas! and Wo, wo! over the loss of vocations, and the disappointment of hopes, and the scorn of God's love, and the ruin of souls. One generation succeeds another, and whenever they look down upon earth from their golden thrones, they see scarcely anything but a multitude of guardian spirits, downcast and sad, each following his own charge, in anxiety, or in terror, or in despair, vainly endeavoring to shield him from the enemy, and failing because he will not be shielded. Times come and go, and man will not believe, that that is to be which is not yet, or that what now is only continues for a season, and is not eternity. The end is the trial; the world passes; it is but a pageant and a scene; the lofty palace crumbles, the busy city is mute, the ships of Tarshish have sped away. On heart and flesh death is coming; the veil is breaking. Departing soul, how hast thou used thy talents, thy opportunities, the light poured around thee, the warnings given thee, the grace inspired into thee? Oh, my Lord and Savior, support me in that hour in the strong arms of Thy sacraments, and by the fresh fragrance of Thy consolations. Let the absolving words be said over me, and the holy oil sign and seal me, and Thy own body be my food, and Thy blood my sprinkling; and let my sweet mother Mary breathe on me, and my angel whisper peace to me, and my glorious saints, and my own dear father, Philip, smile on me; that in them all, and through them all, I may receive the gift of perseverance, and die, as I desire to live, in Thy faith, in Thy Church, in Thy service, and in Thy love.

BUSHNELL

UNCONSCIOUS INFLUENCE

BIOGRAPHICAL NOTE

Horace Bushnell was born at Litchfield, Connecticut, in 1802. Graduated at Yale 1827. In 1833 he became pastor of the North Congregational Church, Hartford, Conn., resigned in 1859 and died in 1876. He wrote many theological works. Among them "Christian Nurture" (1847), a book now looked upon as of classical authority. Considerable discussion among Calvinists was aroused by his "Nature and the Supernatural," and his "The Vicarious Sacrifice" (1865) as being out of accord with the accepted creeds of the Congregational churches. He lacked the sympathy and dramatic instinct necessary to great oratorical achievement, but his sermons prove by their profound suggestiveness that he was a man of keen spiritual insight, and preached with force and impressiveness. His influence upon the ministers of America in modifying theology and remolding the general type of preaching is fairly comparable with that of Robertson.

BUSHNELL

1802-1876
UNCONSCIOUS INFLUENCE[4]

Then went in also that other disciple.—John xx., 8.

In this slight touch or turn of history, is opened to us, if we scan closely, one of the most serious and fruitful chapters of Christian doctrine. Thus it is that men are ever touching unconsciously the springs of motion in each other; thus it is that one man, without thought or intention, or even a consciousness of the fact, is ever leading some other after him. Little does Peter think, as he comes up where his doubting brother is looking into the sepulcher, and goes straight in, after his peculiar manner, that he is drawing in his brother apostle after him. As little does John think, when he loses his misgivings, and goes into the sepulcher after Peter, that he is following his brother. And just so, unaware to himself, is every man, the whole race through, laying hold of his fellow-man, to lead him where otherwise he would not go. We overrun the boundaries of our personality—we flow together. A Peter leads a John, a John goes after Peter, both of them unconscious of any influence exerted or received. And thus our life and conduct are ever propagating themselves, by a law of social contagion, throughout the circles and times in which we live.

There are, then, you will perceive, two sorts of influence belonging to man; that which is active or voluntary, and that which is unconscious—that which we exert purposely or in

4   From "Sermons for the New Life," published by Charles Scribner's Sons.

179

the endeavor to sway another, as by teaching, by argument, by persuasion, by threatenings, by offers and promises, and that which flows out from us, unaware to ourselves, the same which Peter had over John when he led him into the sepulcher. The importance of our efforts to do good, that is of our voluntary influence, and the sacred obligation we are under to exert ourselves in this way, are often and seriously insisted on. It is thus that Christianity has become, in the present age, a principle of so much greater activity than it has been for many centuries before; and we fervently hope that it will yet become far more active than it now is, nor cease to multiply its industry, till it is seen by all mankind to embody the beneficence and the living energy of Christ Himself.

But there needs to be reproduced, at the same time, and partly for this object, a more thorough appreciation of the relative importance of that kind of influence or beneficence which is insensibly exerted. The tremendous weight and efficacy of this, compared with the other, and the sacred responsibility laid upon us in regard to this, are felt in no such degree or proportion as they should be; and the consequent loss we suffer in character, as well as that which the Church suffers in beauty and strength, is incalculable. The more stress, too, needs to be laid on this subject of insensible influence, because it is insensible; because it is out of mind, and, when we seek to trace it, beyond a full discovery.

If the doubt occur to any of you, in the announcement of this subject, whether we are properly responsible for an influence which we exert insensibly; we are not, I reply, except so far as this influence flows directly from our character and conduct. And this it does, even much more uniformly than our active influence. In the latter we may fail of our end by a want of wisdom or skill, in which case we are still as meritorious, in God's sight, as if we succeeded. So, again, we may really succeed, and do great good by our active endeavors, from motives altogether base and hypocritical, in which case we are as evil, in God's sight, as if we had failed. But the influences we exert unconsciously will almost never disagree with our real character. They are honest influences, following our character, as the shadow follows the sun. And, therefore, we are much more certainly responsible for them, and their effects on the world. They go streaming from us in all directions, tho in channels that we do not see, poisoning or healing around the roots of society, and among the hidden wells of character. If good ourselves, they are good; if bad, they are bad. And, since they reflect so exactly our character, it is impossible to doubt our responsibility for their effects on the world. We must answer not only for what we do with a purpose, but for the influence we exert insensibly. To give you any just impressions of the breadth and seriousness of such a reckoning I know to be impossible. No mind can trace it. But it will be something gained if I am able to awaken only a suspicion of the vast extent and power of those influences, which are ever flowing out unbidden upon society, from your life and character.

In the prosecution of my design, let me ask of you, first of all, to expel the common prejudice that there can be nothing of consequence in unconscious influences, because they make no report, and fall on the world unobserved. Histories and biographies make little account of the power men exert insensibly over each other. They tell how men have led armies, established empires, enacted laws, gained causes, sung, reasoned, and taught—always occupied in setting forth what they do with a purpose. But what they do without purpose, the streams of influence that flow out from their persons unbidden on the world, they can not trace or compute, and seldom even mention. So also the public laws make men responsible only for what they do with a positive purpose, and take no account of the mischiefs or benefits that are communicated by their noxious or healthful example. The same is true in the discipline of families, churches, and schools; they make no account of the things we do, except we will them. What we do insensibly passes for nothing, because no human government can trace such influences with sufficient certainty to make their authors responsible.

But you must not conclude that influences of this kind are insignificant, because they are unnoticed and noiseless. How is it in the natural world? Behind the mere show, the outward noise and stir of the world, nature always conceals her hand of control, and the laws by which she rules. Who ever saw with the eye, for example, or heard with the ear, the exertions of that tremendous astronomic force, which every moment holds the compact of the physical universe together? The lightning is, in fact, but a mere firefly spark in comparison; but, because it glares on the clouds, and thunders so terribly in the ear, and rives the tree or the rock where it falls, many will be ready to think that it is a vastly more potent agent than gravity.

The Bible calls the good man's life a light, and it is the nature of light to flow out spontaneously in all directions, and fill the world unconsciously with its beams. So the Christian shines, it would say, not so much because he will, as because he is a luminous object. Not that the active influence of Christians is made of no account in the figure, but only that this symbol of light has its propriety in the fact that their unconscious influence is the chief influence, and has the precedence in its power over the world. And yet, there are many who will be ready to think that light is a very tame and feeble instrument, because it is noiseless. An earthquake, for example, is to them a much more vigorous and effective agency. Hear how it comes thundering through solid foundations of nature. It rocks a whole continent. The noblest works of man—cities, monuments, and temples— are in a moment leveled to the ground, or swallowed down the opening gulfs of fire. Little do they think that the light of every morning, the soft, and genial, and silent light, is an agent many times more powerful. But let the light of the morning cease and return no more, let the hour of morning come, and bring with it no dawn; the outcries of a horror-stricken world fill the air, and make, as it were, the darkness audible. The beasts go wild and frantic at the loss of the sun. The vegetable growths turn pale and die. A chill creeps on, and frosty winds begin to howl across the freezing earth. Colder, and yet colder, is the night. The vital blood, at length, of all creatures, stops congealed. Down goes the frost toward the earth's center. The heart of the sea is frozen; nay, the earthquakes are themselves frozen in, under their fiery caverns. The very globe itself, too, and all the fellow planets that have lost their sun, are become mere balls of ice, swinging silent in the darkness. Such is the light, which revisits us in the silence of the morning. It makes no shock or scar. It would not wake an infant in his cradle. And yet it perpetually new creates the world, rescuing it each morning, as a prey, from night and chaos. So the Christian is a light, even "the light of the world," and we must not think that, because he shines insensibly or silently, as a mere luminous object, he is therefore powerless. The greatest powers are ever those which lie back of the little stirs and commotion of nature; and I verily believe that the insensible influences of good men are much more potent than what I have called their voluntary, or active, as the great silent powers of nature are of greater consequence than her little disturbances and tumults. The law of human influences is deeper than many suspect, and they lose sight of it altogether. The outward endeavors made by good men or bad to sway others, they call their influence; whereas, it is, in fact, but a fraction, and, in most cases, but a very small fraction, of the good or evil that flows out of their lives. Nay, I will even go further. How many persons do you meet, the insensible influence of whose manners and character is so decided as often to thwart their voluntary influence; so that, whatever they attempt to do, in the way of controlling others, they are sure to carry the exact opposite of what they intend! And it will generally be found that, where men undertake by argument or persuasion to exert a power, in the face of qualities that make them odious or detestable, or only not entitled to respect, their insensible influence will be too strong for them. The total effect of the life is then of a kind directly opposite to the voluntary endeavor, which, of course, does not add so much as a fraction to it.

I call your attention, next, to the twofold powers of effect and expression by which man connects with his fellow man. If we distinguish man as a creature of language, and thus qualified to communicate himself to others, there are in him two sets or kinds of language, one which is voluntary in the use, and one that is involuntary; that of speech in the literal sense, and that expression of the eye, the face, the look, the gait, the motion, the tone of cadence, which is sometimes called the natural language of the sentiments. This natural language, too, is greatly enlarged by the conduct of life, that which, in business and society, reveals the principles and spirit of men. Speech, or voluntary language, is a door to the soul, that we may open or shut at will; the other is a door that stands open evermore, and reveals to others constantly, and often very clearly, the tempers, tastes, and motives of their hearts. Within, as we may represent, is character, charging the common reservoir of influence, and through these twofold gates of the soul pouring itself out on the world. Out of one it flows at choice, and whensoever we purpose to do good or evil to men. Out of the other it flows each moment, as light from the sun, and propagates itself in all beholders.

Then if we go to others, that is, to the subjects of influence, we find every man endowed with two inlets of impression; the ear and the understanding for the reception of speech, and the sympathetic powers, the sensibilities or affections, for tinder to those sparks of emotion revealed by looks, tones, manners and general conduct. And these sympathetic powers, tho not immediately rational, are yet inlets, open on all sides, to the understanding and character. They have a certain wonderful capacity to receive impressions, and catch the meaning of signs, and propagate in us whatsoever falls into their passive molds from others. The impressions they receive do not come through verbal propositions, and are never received into verbal propositions, it may be, in the mind, and therefore many think nothing of them. But precisely on this account are they the more powerful, because it is as if one heart were thus going directly into another, and carrying in its feelings with it. Beholding, as in a glass, the feelings of our neighbor, we are changed into the same image, by the assimilating power of sensibility and fellow-feeling. Many have gone so far, and not without show, at least, of reason, as to maintain that the look or expression, and even the very features of children, are often changed by exclusive intercourse with nurses and attendants. Furthermore, if we carefully consider, we shall find it scarcely possible to doubt, that simply to look on bad and malignant faces, or those whose expressions have become infected by vice, to be with them and become familiarized to them, is enough permanently to affect the character of persons of mature age. I do not say that it must of necessity subvert their character, for the evil looked upon may never be loved or welcomed in practise; but it is something to have these bad images in the soul, giving out their expressions there, and diffusing their odor among the thoughts, as long as we live. How dangerous a thing is it, for example, for a man to become accustomed to sights of cruelty? What man, valuing the honor of his soul, would not shrink from yielding himself to such an influence? No more is it a thing of indifference to become accustomed to look on the manners, and receive the bad expression of any kind of sin.

The door of involuntary communication, I have said, is always open. Of course we are communicating ourselves in this way to others at every moment of our intercourse or presence with them. But how very seldom, in comparison, do we undertake by means of speech to influence others! Even the best Christian, one who most improves his opportunities to do good, attempts but seldom to sway another by voluntary influence, whereas he is all the while shining as a luminous object unawares, and communicating of his heart to the world.

But there is yet another view of this double line of communication which man has with his fellow-men, which is more general, and displays the import of the truth yet more convincingly. It is by one of these modes of communication that we are constituted members of voluntary society, and by the other, parts of a general mass, or members of involuntary society. You are all, in a certain view, individuals, and separate as persons from each other; you are also, in a certain other view, parts of a common body, as truly as the parts of a stone. Thus if you ask how it is that you and all men came without your consent to exist in society, to be within its power, to be under its laws, the answer is, that while you are a man, you are also a fractional element of a larger and more comprehensive being, called society—be it the family, the church, the state. In a certain department of your nature, it is open; its sympathies and feelings are open. On this open side you will adhere together, as parts of a larger nature, in which there is a common circulation of want, impulse, and law. Being thus made common to each other voluntarily, you become one mass, one consolidated social body, animated by one life. And observe how far this involuntary communication and sympathy between the members of a state or a family is sovereign over their character. It always results in what we call the national or family spirit; for there is a spirit peculiar to every state and family in the world. Sometimes, too, this national or family spirit takes a religious or an irreligious character, and appears almost to absorb the religious self-government of individuals. What was the national spirit of France, for example, at a certain time, but a spirit of infidelity? What is the religious spirit of Spain at this moment, but a spirit of bigotry, quite as wide of Christianity and destructive of character as the spirit of falsehood? What is the family spirit in many a house, but the spirit of gain, or pleasure, or appetite, in which everything that is warm, dignified, genial, and good in religion, is visibly absent? Sometimes you will almost fancy that you see the shapes of money in the eyes of children. So it is that we are led on by nations, as it were, to good or bad immortality. Far down in the secret foundations of life and society there lie concealed great laws and channels of influence, which make the race common to each other in all the main departments or divisions of the social mass, laws which often escape our notice altogether, but which are to society as gravity to the general system of God's works.

But these are general considerations, and more fit, perhaps, to give you a rational conception of the modes of influence and their relative power, than to verify that conception, or establish its truth. I now proceed to add, therefore, some miscellaneous proofs of a more particular nature.

And I mention, first of all, the instinct of imitation in children. We begin our mortal experience, not with acts grounded in judgment or reason, or with ideas received through language, but by simple imitation, and, under the guidance of this, we lay our foundations. The child looks and listens, and whatsoever tone of feeling or manner of conduct is displayed around him, sinks into his plastic, passive soul, and becomes a mold of his being ever after. The very handling of the nursery is significant, and the petulance, the passion, the gentleness, the tranquillity indicated by it, are all reproduced in the child. His soul is a purely receptive nature, and that for a considerable period, without choice or selection. A little further on he begins voluntarily to copy everything he sees. Voice, manner, gait, everything which the eye sees, the mimic instinct delights to act over. And thus we have a whole generation of future men, receiving from us their beginnings, and the deepest impulses of their life and immortality. They watch us every moment, in the family, before the hearth, and at the table; and when we are meaning them no good or evil, when we are conscious of exerting no influence over them, they are drawing from us impressions and molds of habit, which, if wrong, no heavenly discipline can wholly remove; or, if right, no bad associations utterly dissipate. Now it may be doubted, I think, whether, in all the active influence of our lives, we do as much to shape the destiny of our fellow-men as we do in this single article of unconscious influence over children.

Still further on, respect for others takes the place of imitation. We naturally desire the approbation or good opinion of others. You see the strength of this feeling in the article of fashion. How few persons have the nerve to resist a fashion! We have fashions, too, in literature, and in worship, and in moral and religious doctrine, almost equally powerful. How many will violate the best rules of society, because it is the practise of the circle! How many reject Christ because of friends or acquaintance, who have no suspicion of the influence they exert, and will not have, till the last days show them what they have done! Every good man has thus a power in his person, more mighty than his words and arguments, and which others feel when he little suspects it. Every bad man, too, has a fund of poison in his character, which is tainting those around him, when it is not in his thoughts to do them injury. He is read and understood. His sensual tastes and habits, his unbelieving spirit, his suppressed leer at religions, have all a power, and take hold of the heart of others, whether he will have it so or not.

Again, how well understood is it that the most active feelings and impulses of mankind are contagious. How quick enthusiasm of any sort is to kindle, and how rapidly it catches from one to another, till a nation blazes in the flame! In the case of the Crusades you have an example where the personal enthusiasm of one man put all the states of Europe in motion. Fanaticism is almost equally contagious. Fear and superstition always infect the mind of the circle in which they are manifested. The spirit of war generally becomes an epidemic of madness, when once it has got possession of a few minds. The spirit of party is propagated in a similar manner. How any slight operation in the market may spread, like a fire, if successful, till trade runs wild in a general infatuation, is well known. Now, in all these examples, the effect is produced, not by active endeavor to carry influence, but mostly by that insensible propagation which follows, when a flame of any kind is once more kindled.

It is also true, you may ask, that the religious spirit propagates itself or tends to propagate itself in the same way? I see no reason to question that it does. Nor does anything in the doctrine of spiritual influences, when rightly understood, forbid the supposition. For spiritual influences are never separated from the laws of thought in the individual, and the laws of feeling and influence in society. If, too, every disciple is to be an "epistle known and read of all men," what shall we expect, but that all men will be somehow affected by the reading? Or if he is to be a light in the world, what shall we look for, but that others, seeing his good works, shall glorify God on his account? How often is it seen, too, as a fact of observation, that one or a few good men kindle at length a holy fire in the community in which they live, and become the leaven of general reformation! Such men give a more vivid proof in their persons of the reality of religious faith than any words or arguments could yield. They are active; they endeavor, of course, to exert a good voluntary influence; but still their chief power lies in their holiness and the sense they produce in others of their close relation to God.

It now remains to exhibit the very important fact, that where the direct or active influence of men is supposed to be great, even this is due, in a principal degree, to that insensible influence by which their arguments, reproofs, and persuasions are secretly invigorating. It is not mere words which turn men; it is the heart mounting, uncalled, into the expression of the features; it is the eye illuminated by reason, the look beaming with goodness; it is the tone of the voice, that instrument of the soul, which changes quality with such amazing facility, and gives out in the soft, the tender, the tremulous, the firm, every shade of emotion and character. And so much is there in this, that the moral stature and character of the man that speaks are likely to be well represented in his manner. If he is a stranger, his way will inspire confidence and attract good will. His virtues will be seen, as it were, gathering round him to minister words and forms of thought, and their voices will be heard in the fall of his cadences. And the same is true of bad men, or men who have nothing in their character corresponding to what they attempt to do. If without heart or interest you attempt to move another, the involuntary man tells what you are doing in a hundred ways at once. A hypocrite, endeavoring to exert a good influence, only tries to convey by words what the lying look, and the faithless affectation, or dry exaggeration of his manner perpetually resists. We have it for a fashion to attribute great or even prodigious results to the voluntary efforts and labors of men. Whatever they effect is commonly referred to nothing but the immediate power of what they do. Let us take an example, like that of Paul, and analyze it. Paul was a man of great fervor and enthusiasm. He combined, withal, more of what is lofty and morally commanding in his character, than most of the very distinguished men of the world. Having this for his natural character, and his natural character exalted and made luminous by Christian faith, and the manifest indwelling of God, he had of course an almost superhuman sway over others. Doubtless he was intelligent, strong in argument, eloquent, active, to the utmost of his powers, but still he moved the world more by what he was than by what he did. The grandeur and spiritual splendor of his character were ever adding to his active efforts an element of silent power, which was the real and chief cause of their efficacy. He convinced, subdued, inspired, and led, because of the half-divine authority which appeared in his conduct, and his glowing spirit. He fought the good fight, because he kept the faith, and filled his powerful nature with influences drawn from higher worlds.

And here I must conduct you to a yet higher example, even that of the Son of God, the light of the world. Men dislike to be swayed by direct, voluntary influence. They are jealous of such control, and are therefore best approached by conduct and feeling, and the authority of simple worth, which seem to make no purposed onset. If goodness appears, they welcome its celestial smile; if heaven descends to encircle them, they yield to its sweetness; if truth appears in the life, they honor it with a secret homage; if personal majesty and glory appear, they bow with reverence, and acknowledge with shame their own vileness. Now it is on this side of human nature that Christ visits us, preparing just that kind of influence which the spirit of truth may wield with the most persuasive and subduing effect. It is the grandeur of His character which constitutes the chief power of His ministry, not His miracles or teachings apart from His character. Miracles were useful, at the time, to arrest attention, and His doctrine is useful at all times as the highest revelation of truth possible in speech; but the greatest truth of the gospel, notwithstanding, is Christ Himself—a human body becomes the organ of the divine nature, and reveals, under the conditions of an earthly life, the glory of God! The Scripture writers have much to say, in this connection, of the image of God; and an image, you know, is that which simply represents, not that which acts, or reasons, or persuades. Now it is this image of God which makes the center, the sun itself, of the gospel. The journeyings, teachings, miracles, and sufferings of Christ, all had their use in bringing out this image, or what is the same, in making conspicuous the character and feelings of God, both toward sinners and toward sin. And here is the power of Christ—it is that God's beauty, love, truth, and justice shines through Him. It is the influence which flows unconsciously and spontaneously out of Christ, as the friend of man, the light of the world, the glory of the Father, made visible. And some have gone so far as to conjecture that God made the human person, originally, with a view to its becoming the organ or vehicle by which He might reveal His communicable attributes to other worlds. Christ, they believe, came to inhabit this organ, that He might execute a purpose so sublime. The human person is constituted, they say, to be a mirror of God; and God, being imaged in that mirror, as in Christ, is held up to the view of this and other worlds. It certainly is to the view of this; and if the Divine nature can use the organ so effectively to express itself unto us, if it can bring itself, through the looks, tones, motions, and conduct of a human person, more close to our sympathies than by any other means, how can we think that an organ so communicative, inhabited by us, is not always breathing our spirit and transferring our image insensibly to others?

I have protracted the argument on this subject beyond what I could have wished, but I can not dismiss it without suggesting a few thoughts necessary to its complete practical effect.

One very obvious and serious inference from it, and the first which I will name, is, that it is impossible to live in this world and escape responsibility. It is not that they alone, as you have seen, who are trying purposely to convert or corrupt others, who exert an influence; you can not live without exerting influence. The doors of your soul are open on others, and theirs on you. You inhabit a house which is well-nigh transparent; and what you are within, you are ever showing yourself to be without, by signs that have no ambiguous expression. If you had the seeds of a pestilence in your body, you would not have a more active contagion than you have in your tempers, tastes, and principles. Simply to be in this world, whatever you are, is to exert an influence—an influence, too, compared with which mere language and persuasion are feeble. You say that you mean well; at least, you think you mean to injure no one. Do you injure no one? Is your example harmless? Is it ever on the side of God and duty? You can not reasonably doubt that others are continually receiving impressions from your character. As little you can doubt that you must answer for these impressions. If the influence you exert is unconsciously exerted, then it is only the most sincere, the truest expression of your character. And for what can you be held responsible, if not for this? Do not deceive yourselves in the thought that you are at least doing no injury, and are, therefore, living without responsibility; first, make it sure that you are not every hour infusing moral death insensibly into your children, wives, husbands, friends, and acquaintances. By a mere look or glance, not unlikely, you are conveying the influence that shall turn the scale of some one's immortality. Dismiss, therefore, the thought that you are living without responsibility; that is impossible. Better is it frankly to admit the truth; and if you will risk the influence of a character unsanctified by duty and religion, prepare to meet your reckoning manfully, and receive the just recompense of reward.

The true philosophy or method of doing good is also here explained. It is, first of all and principally, to be good—to have a character that will of itself communicate good. There must and will be active effort where there is goodness of principle; but the latter we should hold to be the principal thing, the root and life of all. Whether it is a mistake more sad or more ridiculous, to make mere stir synonymous with doing good, we need not inquire; enough, to be sure that one who has taken up such a notion of doing good, is for that reason a nuisance to the Church. The Christian is called a light, not lightning. In order to act with effect on others, he must walk in the Spirit, and thus become the image of goodness; he must be so akin to God, and so filled with His dispositions, that he shall seem to surround himself with a hallowed atmosphere. It is folly to endeavor to make ourselves shine before we are luminous. If the sun without his beams should talk to the planets, and argue with them till the final day, it would not make them shine; there must be light in the sun itself; and then they will shine, of course. And this, my brethren, is what God intends for you all. It is the great idea of His gospel, and the work of His spirit, to make you lights in the world. His greatest joy is to give you character, to beautify your example, to exalt your principles, and make you each the depository of His own almighty grace. But in order to do this, something is necessary on your part—a full surrender of your mind to duty and to God, and a perpetual desire of this spiritual intimacy; having this, having a participation thus of the goodness of God, you will as naturally communicate good as the sun communicates his beams.

Our doctrine of unconscious and undesigning influence shows how it is, also, that the preaching of Christ is often unfruitful, and especially in times of spiritual coldness. It is not because truth ceases to be truth, nor, of necessity, because it is preached in a less vivid manner, but because there are so many influences preaching against the preacher. He is one, the people are many; his attempt to convince and persuade is a voluntary influence;

their lives, on the other hand, and especially the lives of those who profess what is better, are so many unconscious influences ever streaming forth upon the people, and back and forth between each other. He preaches the truth, and they, with one consent, are preaching the truth down; and how can he prevail against so many, and by a kind of influence so unequal? When the people of God are glowing with spiritual devotion to Him, and love to men, the case is different; then they are all preaching with the preacher, and making an atmosphere of warmth for his words to fall in; great is the company of them that publish the truth, and proportionally great its power. Shall I say more? Have you not already felt, my brethren, the application to which I would bring you? We do not exonerate ourselves; we do not claim to be nearer to God or holier than you; but, ah! you know how easy it is to make a winter about us, or how cold it feels! Our endeavor is to preach the truth of Christ and His cross as clearly and as forcefully as we can. Sometimes it has a visible effect, and we are filled with joy; sometimes it has no effect, and then we struggle on, as we must, but under great oppression. Have we none among you that preach against us in your lives? If we show you the light of God's truth, does it never fall on banks of ice; which if the light shows through, the crystal masses are yet as cold as before? We do not accuse you; that we leave to God, and to those who may rise up in the last day to testify against you. If they shall come out of your own families; if they are the children that wear your names, the husband or wife of your affections; if they declare that you, by your example, kept them away from Christ's truth and mercy, we may have accusations to meet of our own, and we leave you to acquit yourselves as best you may. I only warn you, here, of the guilt which our Lord Jesus Christ will impute to them that hinder His gospel.

END OF VOLUME IV.